my revision notes

Edexcel **AS**
RELIGIOUS STUDIES FOUNDATIONS
PHILOSOPHY OF RELIGION AND ETHICS

Gordon Reid

HODDER EDUCATION

Scripture quotations are taken form *The Holy Bible, New International Version Anglicised*, Copyright © 1979, 1984 by Biblica, Inc. Used by permission of Hodder & Stoughton publishers, a division of Hachette UK Ltd. All rights reserved. "NIV" is a registered trademark of Biblica, Inc. UK trademark number 1448790.

Every effort has been made to trace all copyright holders, but if any have been inadvertently overlooked the Publishers will be pleased to make the necessary arrangements at the first opportunity.

Although every effort has been made to ensure that website addresses are correct at time of going to press, Hodder Education cannot be held responsible for the content of any website mentioned in this book. It is sometimes possible to find a relocated web page by typing in the address of the home page for a website in the URL window of your browser.

Hachette Livre UK's policy is to use papers that are natural, renewable and recyclable products and made from wood grown in sustainable forests. The logging and manufacturing processes are expected to conform to the environmental regulations of the country of origin.

Orders: please contact Bookpoint Ltd, 130 Milton Park, Abingdon, Oxon OX14 4SB. Telephone: +44 (0)1235 827720. Fax: +44 (0)1235 400454. Lines are open 9.00a.m.–5.00p.m., Monday to Saturday, with a 24-hour message answering service. Visit our website at www.hoddereducation.co.uk

© Gordon Reid 2013
First published in 2013 by
Hodder Education,
An Hachette UK Company
London NW1 3BH

Impression number   10 9 8 7 6 5 4 3 2
Year   2017 2016 2015 2014 2013

Cover photo © Ben Hung/iStockphoto
Typeset in CronosPro-Lt 12/14 points by Datapage (India) Pvt. Ltd.
Printed in India

A catalogue record for this title is available from the British Library
ISBN 978 1 444 182439

Get the most from this book

Everyone has to decide his or her own revision strategy, but it is essential to review your work, learn it and test your understanding. These Revision Notes will help you do that in a planned way, topic by topic. They cover the two areas of Unit 1 Foundations (6RS01) Area A: Philosophy of Religion and Area B: Ethics. Use this book as the cornerstone of your revision and don't hesitate to write in it – personalise your notes and check your progress by ticking off each section as you revise.

☑ **Tick to track your progress**

Use the revision planner on pages 4 and 5 to plan your revision, topic by topic. Tick each box when you have:

● revised and understood a topic
● tested yourself
● practised the exam questions and gone online to check your answers.

You can also keep track of your revision by ticking off each topic heading in the book. You may find it helpful to add your own notes as you work through each topic.

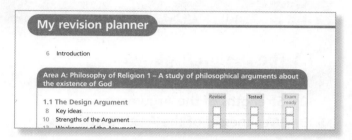

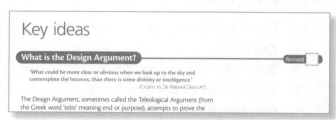

Features to help you succeed

Exam tips

Throughout the book there are tips to help you boost your final grade.

Typical mistakes

Identifies the typical mistakes candidates make and explains how you can avoid them.

Now test yourself

These short, knowledge-based questions provide the first step in testing your learning. Check your answers at the back of the book.

Key words

Clear, concise definitions of essential key terms are provided on the page where they appear.

Key quotes

Quotations from key scholars concisely express key ideas or views relevant to each topic.

Exam practice

Exam-style questions are provided for each topic. Use them to consolidate your revision and practise your exam skills.

Online

Go online to check your answers to the exam questions at www.therevisionbutton.co.uk/myrevisionnotes

My revision planner

Introduction

What is Philosophy of Religion about?

Philosophy of Religion covers some of the deepest and most important questions that have ever been asked – questions like 'Is there a God?', 'What might God be like?' 'Has science replaced religion?' 'Do miracles happen?' and 'Why is there so much evil and suffering in the world?'

What is Ethics about?

Ethics looks at the kind of people we are and what we mean by right and wrong/ good and bad. It asks question such as 'How do we choose right from wrong?', 'Is morality linked to religion?', 'Why do we make the choices that we do?'

Philosophy of Religion and Ethics examine and evaluate questions like these.

Studying these subjects will help you to develop:

- an interest and enthusiasm for philosophy, religion and the wider world
- an interest in how we make ethical and moral decisions
- your knowledge, understanding and evaluative skills
- an enquiring, critical and reflective mind
- your own views and opinions

What is covered in AS Philosophy of Religion and Ethics?

Unit 1 Area A: Philosophy of Religion

1 Philosophical arguments about the existence of God:
- Design – key ideas, strengths and weaknesses
- Cosmological – key ideas, strengths and weaknesses
2 Selected problems in the philosophy of religion:
- Problems of evil and suffering, different types of problems and solutions
- A study of philosophical debates about miracles: concepts of miracle; reasons to believe in miracles; philosophical problems with reference to Hume

Unit 1 Area B: Ethics

1 Ethical concepts:
- The relationship between religion and morality.
- Utilitarianism
- Situation Ethics
2 Ethical dilemmas:
- Issues of war and peace
- Sexual ethics

How are AO1 and AO2 assessed?

Candidates answer three questions. They must study two units and may not answer more than two questions from the same unit.

The external examination is 1 hour and 45 minutes. The total number of marks is 30 per question and 90 overall. The 30 marks are made up of 21 for AO1 and 9 for AO2.

For AO1 candidates are expected to:

- Select and demonstrate clearly relevant knowledge and understanding

- Use evidence and examples to explain key ideas
- Use correct, clear language and terminology
- Use relevant and accurate information
- Identify important features

For AO2 candidates are expected to:

- Critically evaluate and justify a point of view
- Analyse alternative views
- Use evidence and reasoned argument
- Express issues clearly, using appropriate vocabulary

Exam practice answer guidance at **www.therevisionbutton.co.uk/myrevisionnotes**

Countdown to my exams

6–8 weeks to go

- Start by looking at the specification available from **www.edexcel.com**. Make sure you know exactly what material you need to revise and the style of the examination. Use the revision planner on pages 4 and 5 to familiarise yourself with the topics.

- Organise your notes, making sure you have covered everything on the specification. The revision planner will help you group your notes into topics.

- Work out a realistic revision plan that will allow you time for relaxation. Set aside days and times for all the subjects that you need to study, and stick to your timetable.

- Set yourself sensible targets. Break your revision down into focused sessions of around 40 minutes, divided by breaks. These Revision Notes organise the basic facts into short, memorable sections to make revising easier.

Revised ☐

4–6 weeks to go

- Read through the relevant sections of this book and refer to the exam tips, typical mistakes and key words. Tick off the topics as you feel confident about them. Highlight those topics you find difficult and look at them again in detail.

- Test your understanding of each topic by working through the 'Now test yourself' questions in the book. Look up the answers at the back of the book.

- Make a note of any problem areas as you revise, and ask your teacher to go over these in class.

- Look at past papers. They are one of the best ways to revise and practise your exam skills. Write or prepare planned answers to the exam practice questions provided in this book. Check your answers online at www.therevisionbutton.co.uk/myrevisionnotes

- Try different revision methods. For example, you can make notes using mind maps, spider diagrams or flash cards.

- Track your progress using the revision planner and give yourself a reward when you have achieved your target.

Revised ☐

One week to go

- Try to fit in at least one more timed practice of an entire past paper and seek feedback from your teacher, comparing your work closely with the mark scheme.

- Check the revision planner to make sure you haven't missed out any topics. Brush up on any areas of difficulty by talking them over with a friend or getting help from your teacher.

- Attend any revision classes put on by your teacher. Remember, he or she is an expert at preparing people for examinations.

Revised ☐

The day before the examination

- Flick through these Revision Notes for useful reminders, for example the examiner's tips, typical mistakes and key words.

- Check the time and place of your examination.

- Make sure you have everything you need – extra pens and pencils, tissues, a watch, bottled water, sweets.

- Allow some time to relax and have an early night to ensure you are fresh and alert for the examinations.

Revised ☐

My exams

AS Unit 1 Religious Studies – Foundations 6RSO1 Area A: Philosophy of Religion

Date: ....

Time: ....

Location:..

AS Unit 1 Religious Studies – Foundations 6RSO1 Area B: Ethics

Date: ....

Time: ....

Location:..

1.1 The Design Argument

Key ideas

What is the Design Argument? Revised

'What could be more clear or obvious when we look up to the sky and contemplate the heavens, than there is some divinity or intelligence.'

(Cicero, in *De Natura Deorum*)

The Design Argument, sometimes called the Teleological Argument (from the Greek word '*telos*' meaning end or purpose), attempts to prove the existence of God by reference to the process of creation.

The Design Argument is one of cause and effect. It claims that certain phenomena within the universe display appear to have been designed (cause) in so far as they are perfectly adapted to fulfil their function (effect). Such design cannot come about by chance and can only be explained with reference to an intelligent, personal designer.

We can, therefore, draw an analogy between the works of human design and the works of nature. There are sufficient similarities between the two to suggest the same cause and effect – design leading to function or purpose. Since the works of nature are far greater than the works of humanity, an infinitely greater designer must exist, which points towards the existence of God.

Cause and effect are easy to see in the world, but how do we explain the cause and effect evident in the universe? Supporters of the Design Argument maintain that scientific explanations for the creation and order of the universe are not complete explanations. This does not mean that scientific explanations of the universe and its features are to be rejected: rather, like an analogy, they point us towards the truth but they are not the whole story. For believers, only God offers a complete explanation. Richard Swinburne writes:

'So there is our universe. It is characterized by vast, all persuasive temporal order, the conformity of nature to formula, recorded in the scientific laws formulated by humans. It started off in such a way ... as to lead to the evolution of animals and humans ... Note that I am not postulating a 'God of the gaps', a god merely to explain the things which science has not yet explained.'

Key features of the Design Argument Revised

- It is an *a posteriori* argument because it uses empirical evidence, from our observation of the world, to show that aspects of the universe seem to have been designed because they are perfectly adapted to fulfil their function.

> *A posteriori* – an argument based on the evidence of our observation of the world.

Exam practice answer guidance at **www.therevisionbutton.co.uk/myrevisionnotes**

- The Design Argument suggests that such perfect adaption could not have come into existence simply by chance. Instead, they appear to be the work of an intelligent, personal designer, whom some people call God.

- The first form of the argument is **analogical**, drawing an analogy between the world or its parts and objects of human design.

- The second form of the argument is **inductive**, and takes the perspective that the universe demonstrates regular order and motion both in its parts and in the whole.

Supporters of the Design Argument claim that there are a number of crucial features that indicate the existence of an intelligent designer:

- Order — objects and scientific laws operate in a regular way.

- Benefit — the universe provides all that is necessary for life.

- Purpose — objects within the universe appear to be working towards an end or purpose.

- Suitability for human life – the universe provides the right environment for human life.

- Appearance – the beauty of nature and the universe suggests that it is intended for something more than basic survival.

> **Analogical** – an argument based on analogies or similarities – for example, seeing the link between the world and objects of human design.
>
> **Inductive** – an argument based on premises and conclusions, for example, the universe shows order and therefore must have been designed.

Key quote

'These phenomena are clearly things too big for science to explain …. I am postulating a God to explain what science explains; I do not deny that science explains, but I postulate God to explain why science explains.'

(the British philosopher Richard Swinburne, *The Existence of God*)

St Thomas Aquinas

Revised

Catholic theologian St Thomas Aquinas (1225–1274) was a supporter of the Design Argument and it became the fifth of his famous 'Five Ways' to prove the existence of God. In *Summa Theologica* he wrote:

'We see that things which lack knowledge, such as natural bodies, act for an end … it is plain that they achieve their end not fortuitously, but designedly. Now whatever lacks knowledge cannot move towards an end, unless it be directed by some being endowed with knowledge and intelligence … and this being we call God.'

Aquinas' view works like this:

- There is beneficial order in the universe i.e. there are things in the universe that work towards an end or purpose.

- This beneficial order could not happen by chance.

- Objects do not have the intelligence to work towards an end or purpose.

- Therefore, they must be directed by something that does have intelligence.

- Therefore God exists.

Typical mistake

Always remember to consider all sides of the argument. Many students make the mistake of only writing about one side. Here, for instance, there are a couple of unanswered questions such as: who establishes that there is beneficial order in the universe? How do we argue from that to the conclusion that God has designed it?

Strengths of the Argument

Immanuel Kant

German philosopher Immanuel Kant (1724–1804) regarded the Design Argument as good because:

- It is an a posteriori one and based on the **empirical** nature of the universe.
- The actions of the universe and its inhabitants could not be explained by the universe itself, and an intelligent designer was the most likely reason.

> **Empirical** – using evidence gained from the senses – touch, smell, sight, taste, sound.

William Paley

English Christian philosopher William Paley's (1743–1805) analogy of the watch (in *Natural Theology*) is a well-known view in support of the argument.

Key quote

'In crossing a heath, suppose I pitched my foot against a stone, and were asked how the stone came to be there, I might possibly answer that, for anything I knew to the contrary, it had lain there for ever; nor would it, perhaps, be very easy to show the absurdity of this answer. But suppose I found a watch upon the ground, and it should be inquired how the watch happened to be in that place, I should hardly think of the answer which I had before given — that, for anything I knew, the watch might always have been there. Yet why should not this answer serve for the watch as well as for the stone? Why is it not as admissible in the second case as in the first? For this reason … when we come to inspect the watch we perceive … that its several parts are framed and put together for a purpose.'

(William Paley, cited in *The Existence of God*)

Paley believed that:

- The world was like a machine, which was made up of parts that worked towards the benefit of the whole.
- This 'machine' works in a methodical and constant way that could not be the result of sheer chance, towards a particular end or goal.
- This is proof of an **intelligent design**.

> **Intelligent design** – the universe shows evidence of having been thought-out in its design.

Paley's view was that if we found a stone on the ground, we might just think it had always been there. However, if we came across a watch, we would think differently because:

- It has a purpose.
- It works in a specific way.
- It has regularity and order.
- Therefore, it must have been designed.

Exam tip

Make sure that you write your examination answer in full sentences. Use bullet points sparingly!

Typical mistake

Remember to always question the evidence. In this case, that means don't tell the story of Paley and the watch. Instead add useful detail to the argument, such as 'Paley accepted that the watch analogy could serve only to demonstrate that there was a designer, and that it does not tell us anything about the nature of the designer'.

Richard Swinburne

Revised ☐

Swinburne also argued strongly in support of the Design Argument. He claimed that:

- The way the universe fits perfectly for the development of human life is just what would be expected from a loving creator.
- God is the best explanation for this creator because of the providential nature of the universe – it contains everything necessary for human survival (air, water, food) within it.

Swinburne said that there are seven features of the universe which increase the likelihood of the universe being designed:

- The existence of the universe.
- The existence of order in the universe.
- The existence of consciousness.
- Human opportunities to be morally good.
- The pattern of history.
- Miracles.
- Religious experience.

It is possible to argue that God created the laws which govern **natural selection** because, through them, human beings and animals would evolve. Richard Swinburne in 'The Existence of God' maintains:

> 'The very success of science in showing us how deeply orderly the natural world is, provides strong grounds for believing that there is an even deeper cause of that order.'

Swinburne argues that:

- Everything in the universe works together in an orderly way ('regularity of co-presence').
- The orderly pattern of the universe is very simple ('regularity of succession').
- The easiest and most simple explanation for the universe is that it has a cosmic designer ('perspective of probability').

Exam tip

Quotations like these really give an examination answer depth – and extra marks!

> 'God being omnipotent is able to produce a world orderly in these respects. And he has a good reason to choose to do so: a world containing human persons is a good thing ... God being perfectly good, is generous. He wants to share.'
>
> (Richard Swinburne)

Natural selection – the biological process by which certain animals become more or less common due to genetic characteristics and changes.

Typical mistake

When using a quotation, don't forget to name the scholar who said it to reinforce your answers. Learn some easy but useful ones such as this one from Swinburne:

> 'To postulate a trillion, trillion other universes rather than one God in order to explain the orderliness of our universe, seems the height of irrationality.'

F. R. Tennant

English theologian F. R. Tennant (1866–1957) supported the Design Argument by claiming that:

● The existence of an intelligent designer is found not just in the order of the universe, but in its beauty – nature, music, art and literature. This is the **aesthetic principle**.

● The universe is more than just orderly; it possesses a natural beauty beyond that which is necessary to live. He observes:

> 'Nature is not just beautiful in places; it is saturated with beauty — on the telescopic and microscopic scale. Our scientific knowledge brings us no nearer to understanding the beauty of music. From an intelligibility point of view, beauty seems to be superfluous and to have little survival value.'

(Tennant in *Philosophical Theology*, 1985)

> **Aesthetic principle** – the beauty in the world is proof of intelligent design.

John Polkinghorne

British theologian Polkinghorne (b. 1930) argued that:

● The beauty of **natural laws** suggest that they did not just happen by chance.

● The universe is not fixed and unchanging, but that God interacts with creation by 'conducting the improvised performance of the universe'.

● The very existence and nature of the physical universe is proof of the existence of a designer. This is the **anthropic principle**.

● God is the 'total explanation' for the design of the universe.

> **Natural laws** – the laws of nature, upon which science is based, that govern the way the universe seems to operate.
>
> **Anthropic principle** – the world was designed to support human life.

Typical mistake

Don't just use random quotations. A short, perceptive quotation can rescue a tired answer. Try this:

> 'It seems to be natural to believe that the rational order and beauty is an expression of a divine mind, and the finely tuned fruitfulness is an expression of divine purpose.'

(Polkinghorne, 'Testing God: Killing the Creator', 1995)

Stephen Hawking

More recently, theoretical physicist Stephen Hawking (b. 1942) argued that:

● Evolution could allow for the existence of God as an intelligent designer because evolution could be the mechanism through which God's creation took place.

● In *A Brief History of Time* (1992) he wrote:

> 'If we do discover a complete theory, it should in time be understandable in broad principle by everyone, not just a few scientists. Then we shall all ... be able to take part in the discussion of the question of why it is that we and the universe exist. If we find the answer to that, then ... we would know the mind of God.'

Weaknesses of the Argument

The main weakness of the Design Argument is that it is based on:

- The human notion of design. However, the universe was not created by humans, so we cannot know that it was designed.
- The assumption that the universe works in an orderly way.

David Hume

In his works *An Enquiry Concerning Human Understanding* and *Dialogues Concerning Natural Religion* (1998), Scottish philosopher David Hume (1711–1776) argued that:

- Paley's watch analogy was unsound, since we have no certain knowledge of the universe in the way that we do have certain knowledge of the watch.
- The universe is unique and cannot be compared to anything else and certainly not to a watch.
- Whilst we might agree that parts of the universe appear to have a purpose, how do we know for certain?
- This leads to **anthropomorphism** where, in this case, God's qualities and characteristics are identified with those of humans.
- If God is compared with a human designer then it serves only to limit his powers.
- If the universe is designed, then it is very poorly designed.
- No supreme designer would have created a universe with so much suffering. Hume observed: 'The world is very faulty and imperfect … it is the work only of some inferior deity.'

> **Anthropomorphism** – attributing human characteristics to concepts, objects or other animals.

Now test yourself

Tested

4 What is the aesthetic principle?
5 What is anthropomorphism?
6 What is the analogical argument?
7 What is the anthropic principle?

Answers on page 61

> **Exam tip**
> Try to end questions with good evidence and argument. For instance, you can sum up Hume's views by saying that the presence of order could be explained without reference to God. There may be grounds for saying that the designer was very powerful and highly intelligent, but need not be God.

Charles Darwin

Revised

In his work *On the Origin of Species by Means of Natural Selection* (1859), English naturalist Charles Darwin (1809–1882) formulated the theory of evolution, which offered an alternative explanation to the Design Argument. After the publication of *The Descent of Man* (1871), supporters of Darwin claimed that his theory proved that the Design Argument was wrong because:

- Life developed in evolutionary steps.
- Living things change and adapt to fit in with the environment. The environment was not made by God for living things.
- There is too much suffering in the natural world for it to have been made by a kind and loving God.

A very effective way to consider all sides of an argument is to question that the views of some famous scholars, such as Darwin, may be wrong. Keep an open mind. For instance, critics of Darwin say he is wrong because:

● He fails to answer the question of why there is life at all.

● There are gaps in fossil records meaning that there is a lack of empirical evidence to support Darwin's theory.

Richard Dawkins

Revised ☐

British evolutionary biologist Richard Dawkins (b. 1941) criticised the Design Argument. He believed that:

● The universe evolved as a series of chances.

● The design of the universe does not show its purpose.

● In the television programme, The Root of all Evil (Channel Four, 2006), Richard Dawkins claimed that creation has nothing to do with God and that 'we are so grotesquely lucky to be here'.

Exam tip

Dawkins is a very popular modern scholar and most examiners will expect students to use him. Try a helpful quotation that adds depth and insight to your answer to illustrate a point, for instance, Dawkins believes that **natural selection** does not require an intelligent designer:

'Natural selection ... has no vision, no foresight, no sight at all. If it can be said to play the role of the watchmaker in nature, it is the blind watchmaker'.

(*The Blind Watchmaker*, 1986)

Natural selection – the biological process by which certain animals become more or less common due to genetic characteristics and changes.

Evil and suffering

Revised ☐

The existence of evil and suffering is an important challenge to the Design Argument:

● In *Nature and Utility in Religion* (quoted in Hick, 1973), J. S. Mill argued the designer of the universe must be very limited in power to allow such suffering.

● If God was indeed the creator, then he must be either limited in power or not all-loving. Mill: 'If the Maker of the world can do all that he will, he wills misery and there is no escaping that conclusion.'

Typical mistake

The argument from evil and suffering is a major topic in its own right. Don't spend too much time explaining it here.

Conclusion

Although the Design Argument has existed for thousands of years, it offers no actual proof and is based on many assumptions. It succeeds in proving that the universe is very probably ordered, so that the universe may have been designed.

Exam tip

Always save a good quotation for the end of your answer, like this:

In *Critique of Pure Reason* (1999) Kant said of the argument:

> 'This proof always deserves to be mentioned with respect. It is the oldest, the clearest and the most accordant with the common reason of mankind.'

Summary

- ✔ The Design Argument is an a posteriori, analytical and inductive argument.
- ✔ It suggests that the universe is the work of an intelligent designer (God).
- ✔ The supporting evidence includes a sense of order and purpose in the way the universe works.
- ✔ The universe works with beneficial order (Aquinas).
- ✔ The workings of the universe are like those of a watch (Paley).
- ✔ The universe works in a providential way (Swinburne).
- ✔ Lack of proof is one criticism of this argument.
- ✔ Another criticism is its reliance on anthropomorphism – attributing human characteristics to non-humans such as God.
- ✔ The universe may be the result of random chance (Dawkins).
- ✔ The existence of evil and suffering suggests there is no intelligent designer.

Exam practice

(a) Examine the key ideas of the Design Argument.

(b) To what extent is it a convincing proof of the existence of God?

Answer guidance online

Online

1.2 The Cosmological Argument

Key ideas

What is the Cosmological Argument?
Revised ☐

The Cosmological Argument comes from the Greek word 'cosmos' meaning universe.

Key features of the Cosmological Argument
Revised ☐

- It uses evidence from the physical world to prove that God exists.
- The Argument is that the universe cannot be explained without reference to causes and factors outside itself.
- The universe is contingent and only the existence of a first, **necessary cause** and mover can really explain its origin.
- The Cosmological Argument is a posteriori.
- The argument assumes that the universe comes into existence by the action of an external agent whom we call 'God'.
- It is an a posteriori argument because it is based on empirical evidence.

> **Necessary cause** – a cause that cannot not exist.
>
> **Complete explanation** – one which explains all the factors are to which nothing more can be added.

The Cosmological Argument declares that God is the ultimate, **complete explanation** for the universe. It is based on the following premise:

- There is something rather than nothing.
- The universe possesses form. The universe did not bring itself into existence.
- A cause was therefore necessary for the universe to come into existence.
- Only this can explain the regularity and purpose of the universe.
- The universe cannot go back forever (infinite regress). It must have a starting point.

Key quote

'A may be explained by B, and B by C, but in the end there will be some one object on whom all other objects depend ... Theism claims that every other object which exists is caused to exist and kept in existence by just one substance, God ... There could in this respect be no simpler explanation than one which postulated only one cause.'

(Richard Swinburne, *The Existence of God*)

Exam tip

Don't forget to use a scholarly quotation to support your answer. It will add insight and understanding to your answer.

The Five Ways of St Thomas Aquinas

Revised

In the *Summa Theologica*, Aquinas suggested 'Five Ways' to prove the existence of God. The first three ways were Cosmological Arguments.

The First Way — from motion

'It is certain, and evident to our senses, that in the world some things are in motion. Now whatever is moved is moved by another ... But this cannot go on to infinity, because then there would be no first mover, and, subsequently, no other mover ... Therefore it is necessary to arrive at a first mover, moved by no other; and this everyone understands to be God.'

(Thomas Aquinas, *Summa Theologica*, Third Article, 'Whether God Exists', cited in Hick (ed.), 1964)

Aquinas argues that:

- Nothing can move itself, it needs to be moved by something else.
- There cannot be an **infinite chain of movers** that has no beginning.
- There must be a first mover that causes motion in all things.
- This first mover we call God.

The Second Way — from cause

'The Second Way is from the nature of efficient cause. In the world of sensible things we find there is an order of efficient causes. Therefore it is necessary to admit to a first efficient cause, to which everyone gives the name of God.'

Here, Aquinas is saying:

- all things are caused
- nothing can be its own cause
- therefore there must be a first cause (God) on which all other causes depend
- God is therefore the first cause of all things.

The Third Way — from necessity and contingency

'The Third Way is taken from possibility and necessity ... we cannot but admit the existence of some being having of itself its own necessity, and not receiving it from another, but rather causing in others their necessity. This all men speak of as God.'

Aquinas' Third Way can be summarised as:

- Everything in the universe is dependent upon factors beyond itself (contingent).
- Those factors themselves depend on other factors (for example, humans depend on the availability of food, air and water to survive).
- There must be a **necessary being** (God), dependent on nothing.
- God exists necessarily and not contingently.

Now test yourself

Tested

1 What is a necessary being?
2 What was Aquinas' Second Way?

Answers on page 61

Infinite chain of movers – a line of movers that goes back forever, without beginning or end.

Potentiality – what might happen.

Actuality – what does happen.

Exam tip

Try to use helpful examples to explain your points. These will show the examiner that you understand the theory and can apply it to reality. For instance, Aquinas believed that motion was 'the reduction of something from **potentiality** to **actuality**'. Fire, for instance, turns wood which is potentially hot into actually being hot. However, something (a third party) must start things off (e.g. light the fire). This is called the 'efficient cause' or 'initiator of change'. Aquinas said that this was God.

Typical mistake

Be careful always to back up what you say with evidence and support from scholars or good examples. Both can be a useful aid to explain your argument and support your viewpoint.

Typical mistake

There are lots of different and important views being expressed here. Don't fall into the trap of trying to write about all the perspectives. It is much better to write about one or two views in depth, with scholarly support, than to write a vague answer covering everything.

Necessary being – a being that must exist and cannot not exist.

Strengths of the Argument

Frederick Copleston
Revised ☐

Catholic philosopher and theologian Frederick Copleston (1907–1994) supported the Cosmological Argument by saying that there could not be an infinite chain of **contingent beings** because they could never have brought themselves into existence:

> 'You see, I don't believe that the infinity of the series of the events ... If you add up chocolates to infinity, you presumably get an infinite number of chocolates. So if you add up contingent beings to infinity, you still get contingent beings, not a necessary being. An infinite series of contingent beings will be, to my way of thinking, as unable to cause itself as one contingent being.'

Copleston's view was:

- everything that exists is caused to exist by an external cause,
- therefore the universe must have been caused to exist by an external cause,
- that cause must not depend on anything else (non-contingent),
- it is, therefore, a 'necessary being',
- it is God.

> **Contingent being** – one which comes in and out of existence or need not have existed e.g. a human being.

Gottfried Leibniz
Revised ☐

German philosopher Gottfried Leibniz (1646–1716) in *Theodicy* (1988) supported the Cosmological Argument by claiming that:

- If the universe had always been in existence, it would still need a 'sufficient reason' for its existence.
- Infinite regress will never offer a complete explanation.
- There is nothing within the universe to show why it exists, so the reason for its existence must lie outside of it.

> **Exam tip**
> Students rarely use a good range of different scholars. Leibniz is a good, slightly different scholar who is well worth using. Try this: 'If you suppose the world eternal, you will suppose nothing but a succession of states, and will not find in any of them a sufficient reason.'

Richard Swinburne
Revised ☐

Swinburne (1996) claimed that the most convincing aspect of the Cosmological Argument was the fact that things actually exist at all:

- It is extraordinary that there should exist anything at all.
- The most natural state of affairs is simply nothing.
- But there is something – so many things.
- If we can explain the many bits of the universe by one simple being which keeps them in existence, we should do so.

> **Typical mistake**
> Many candidates make their examination answers very difficult for the examiner to understand because they put their arguments into one long paragraph, which is then very complicated to follow. Instead, try to use short, crisp paragraphs, each covering just one main point. The examiner will find it much easier to credit you with marks if you answer in this way.

> **Exam tip**
> Don't be afraid to comment on current issues, for instance, here you might say that the Cosmological Argument still finds support in modern science today. The **Big Bang theory** itself proposes a beginning point for the universe, not an infinite regress of events. This shows that you can show how these theories are still relevant.

> **Big Bang theory** – the view that the universe developed from rapid heating and cooling, which led to the formation of matter.

The Kalam Argument

The Cosmological Argument has an Islamic form, known as the Kalam Argument, proposed by al-Kindi (*c.* 801–813 CE) and al-Ghazali (*c.* 1058–1111). The Argument centres around the view that:

- Everything that comes into being must have a cause.
- The universe came into being.
- The universe must have a cause.
- The cause exists without having been caused by something else.
- The cause is a non-physical one.
- God is the cause.

> **Typical mistake**
>
> It is not enough to only write about one form of the Cosmological Argument. Try to use a variety of approaches, such as the Kalam Argument, to reinforce your answer.

William Craig

Craig in *The Kalam Cosmological Argument* (1979) highlighted the importance of the concept of time;

> 'If the universe began to exist, and if the universe is caused, then the cause of the universe must be a personal being who freely chooses to create the world ... the kalam cosmological argument leads to a personal creator of the universe.'

His view was:

- the present moment exists,
- therefore time cannot be infinite,
- this means the universe must have had a start,
- the universe must have been caused to exist,
- this cause is called God,
- if God chose to create the world, then God must be a personal being.

> **Now test yourself**
>
> 3 What is a contingent being?
> 4 What is the main principle of the Kalam Argument?
> 5 What was Craig's main point?
>
> Answers on page 61

Tested

Weaknesses of the Argument

David Hume

In *Dialogues Concerning Natural Religion* (2006) Hume (1711–1776) dismissed the Cosmological Argument, saying:

- There is no need to presume the need for a cause.
- There is no need to look for an explanation for the whole universe.
- It is sufficient to explain the parts of the universe rather than the whole thing.
- The concept of a necessary first being does not make sense.
- Even if there was such a being, why should it be God?
- The universe is simply outside our experience and we cannot, therefore, draw conclusions about it.
- There is no sufficient evidence to point without doubt to the existence of God.

> **Exam tip**
>
> Hume is an important philosopher. Quotations from his works will always add depth to your answer.

> **Key quote**
>
> 'Did I show you the particular causes of each individual in a collection of twenty particles of matter, I should think it very unreasonable should you afterwards ask me what was the cause of the whole twenty. This is sufficiently explained in explaining the cause of the parts.'
>
> (David Hume)

Bertrand Russell

British philosopher Bertrand Russell (1872–1970) said that:

- There was no need to seek a cause for the universe as a whole.
- The universe simply had no explanation, it is simply there. It is a 'brute fact'.
- To seek for the start of the universe is to attempt to answer 'a question that has no meaning.'
- In 'Why I am not a Christian' (1927) he wrote: '... the universe is just there and that's all.'

> **Exam tip**
>
> Like Hume, Russell is important in his criticisms of the Cosmological Argument. Try to include some of his views.

Anthony Kenny

In *The Five Ways* (1965), British philosopher Anthony Kenny (b. 1931) criticised the Cosmological Argument's view that nothing moves by itself. He said:

- Animals and humans move.
- Newton's first law of motion states that movement can be explained by the body's own inertia from previous motion.

Richard Dawkins

Dawkins dismissed the Cosmological Argument saying that:

- It is an 'intellectual non-explanation'.
- If science doesn't provide the answer, then we must do better science.
- We should not seek the answer in guesswork, mythology and speculation.

> **Key quote**
>
> Stephen Hawking in his book *A Brief History of Time* (1988) offered support to the argument:
>
> 'The laws of the universe do not tell us what the universe should have looked like when it started – it would still be up to God to wind up the clockwork and choose how to start it off. So long as the universe had a beginning, we could suppose it had a creator.'

> **Typical mistake**
>
> Although students love to quote from Dawkins, they don't always explain the meaning or importance of the quotation they use. Here, if you use Dawkins' words 'intellectual non-explanation', explain that it means the Cosmological Argument seems a good intellectual argument but, in Dawkins reality, at least it has no real value as an explanation. Make sure you always know the meaning of a quotation before you use it!

Conclusion

On the positive side, the Cosmological Argument remains a strong *a posteriori* argument, based on empirical evidence. It provides a way of explaining the universe. Richard Swinburne argues that:

> 'God is simpler than anything we can imagine and gives a simple explanation for the system.'

But on the negative side, the Argument cannot explain God; it can only offer God as a possible explanation. Herbert McCabe in *A Modern Cosmological Argument* (1980) observed:

> 'The question is: is there an unanswered question about the existence of the world? Can we be puzzled by the existence of the world instead of nothing? I can be and am; and this is to be puzzled about God.'

At this point it is important to remember there are many differing views about the exact nature of God. Here are the main views in the Western tradition:

- Theists – God exists in reality. He created and sustains the universe. He is all-powerful, all-loving and can be known to humans through prayer and religious experiences.

- Deists – God exists in a transcendent way and does not have any interaction with humans.

- Pantheists – God is the universe and the universe is God. God has no direct relationship with humans and cannot be known by them.

- Panentheists – God contains the universe within Himself, and cannot be known by humans.

Now test yourself

Tested

6 Why did Hume say that we cannot draw conclusions about the universe?

7 What was McCabe's view?

8 Why did religious views about the Cosmological Argument dismay Dawkins?

Answers on page 61

Summary

- The cosmological argument is an *a posteriori* argument based on empirical evidence.
- It Shows regularity, order and purpose.
- God is the ultimate, complete explanation.
- God is the first cause/mover.
- God is a necessary being.
- It is covered by Aquinas' Five Ways.
- A slightly different approach is found in the Kalam Argument.
- But why should we look for an ultimate cause?
- The Cosmological Argument is illogical.
- There is a lack of clear scientific evidence

Exam practice

(a) Examine the strengths of the Cosmological Argument.

(b) To what extent is it a convincing proof of the existence of God?

Answer guidance online

Online

2.1 The problem of evil and suffering

Key ideas

Evil and suffering pose a great challenge to the issue of whether or not God exists. We see and hear about terrible evil and suffering all over the world, both **natural** and **moral**. It raises one of the most difficult of all questions: does the occurrence of evil and suffering show that there is no such thing as a loving God? The problem of evil is, according to Hume, 'the rock of atheism'.

Early Christian scholar St Augustine (354–430 CE) summed up the problem. He wrote:

> 'Either God cannot abolish evil or he will not: if he cannot then he is not all-powerful; if he will not, then he is not all good.'
>
> (Confessions)

More recently, Richard Swinburne claimed that evil and suffering were a challenge to religious faith:

> 'There is a problem about why God allows evil, and if the theist does not have a satisfactory answer to it, then his belief in God is less than rational.'
>
> (The Existence of God, 2004)

> **Natural evil** – problems in the natural world, which lead to tsunamis, earthquakes and famines.
>
> **Moral evil** – the results of human action such as murder or theft.

Exam tip

Try to use a good real-life example to support your answers, like this:

The sheer scale of evil and suffering challenges the existence of a loving God. Holocaust survivor Elie Wiesel declared:

> 'Never shall I forget that smoke. Never shall I forget the little faces of the children ... never shall I forget those flames which consumed my faith forever ... never shall I forget those moments which murdered my God and my soul ...'

The problem of evil challenges the concept of the all-loving, all-powerful Creator God of Christianity, Judaism and Islam. It may be summarised as:

- If God created the universe out of nothing, then he is all-powerful (omnipotent).
- He could, therefore, have created a universe that is free from evil and suffering.
- God is omniscient and knows everything.
- He must, therefore, know how to stop evil and suffering.
- He is all-loving (omnibenevolent) and, therefore, would wish to end all evil and suffering. He would not want his creation to suffer.
- Yet evil and suffering exist, so either God is not omnipotent or omnibenevolent *or* he does not exist.
- This is sometimes called the '**inconsistent triad**'.

> **Inconsistent triad** – God is all-loving and all-powerful, yet evil exists.

The problem is known as the 'inconsistent triad':

- God is (a) omnipotent/omniscient and (b) all-loving.
- However, (c) evil exists.
- This means that either (a) or (b) must be logically inconsistent and therefore wrong.

David Hume, in *Dialogues Concerning Natural Religion* (2006), agreed:

- either God is not omnipotent/omniscient, or
- God is not omnibenevolent, or
- evil does not exist, and
- since evil does exist, then God does not.

In a similar way, British theologian Anthony Flew (1923–2010) criticised religious believers who carried on believing in a loving God despite the existence of evil and suffering:

'Now it often seems to people who are not religious as if there was no conceivable event ... the occurrence of which would be admitted by sophisticated religious people to be a sufficient reason for conceding ... "God does not really love us."'

Exam tip

In order to give your answer balance, when you deal with controversial issues try to highlight the views of two different scholars, like this: St Thomas Aquinas in *Summa Theologica* wrote:

'But the name of God means that He is infinite goodness. If, therefore, God existed, there would be no evil discoverable; but there is evil in the world. Therefore God does not exist.'

Solutions to the problem

- A punishment from God. St Augustine believed that humans carry the sin of Adam and must bear the consequences of his wrong-doing.
- An illusion. Mary Baker Eddy, the founder of the Christian Science Movement, said that God was completely good and that only goodness was real. Evil and suffering are simply the failure to understanding the loving nature of God.
- Perspective. If no one is in danger, then a volcano erupting can be seen as a beauty of nature. However, if lives are lost, then it becomes a natural disaster.
- A test of faith. God may allow suffering in a person's life in order to test and strengthen their faith.
- God's plan. God may be all-loving and all-powerful, yet allows evil to exist as part of his greater plan of love.

Now test yourself

1. Give two examples of moral evil.
2. What is the inconsistent triad?
3. In what sense may suffering be seen as a test of faith?

Answers on page 61

Tested

Typical mistake

Remember to write your examination answer in full sentences and remember to define the terms you use. This will show the examiner that you know the material.

Augustinian theodicy

In *Confessions* and *De Genesi ad Litteram*, St Augustine said that evil and suffering do not disprove the existence of an all-loving God because:

- God is good.
- God created a world that was perfectly good.
- The Bible supports this: 'God saw all that he had made, and it was very good' (Genesis 1:31).
- Evil is the going-wrong of something that is good.
- Evil did not come from God. It came from the decisions made by beings to whom God had given free will (angels and humans) and who, as a result, had chosen to turn away from God.
- This is shown in the story of Adam and Eve: 'For God knows that when you eat of it your eyes will be opened and you will be like God, knowing good and evil' (Genesis 3:3–5).

Augustine believed that God's good creation was ruined by human sin and that evil and suffering were the punishment that human beings had brought upon themselves. Christians refer to this as original sin.

As a result, Augustine claimed that:

- God is just and allows suffering to happen as a punishment for human sin.
- Yet as an all-loving God, he sent his son, Jesus Christ, to die so that those who believed could be saved.

Criticisms of Augustinian theodicy

German theologian Schleiermacher (1768–1834), in *The Christian Faith* (1960), said that Augustine was wrong because:

- If God had created a perfectly good world then it could never go wrong.
- If humans were able to choose evil, then evil must have existed in the first place.
- If the world was not perfect to start with, then God is to blame for evil and suffering.
- In nature, suffering is vital for survival; things must die so that others might eat and live. God must have made the world this way.
- God is unjust in allowing humans to be punished for Adam's sin.
- The existence of Hell as a place of eternal punishment contradicts the existence of an all-loving God.
- If Hell was part of the design of the universe, and God knew that the world would go wrong anyway, why did he still allow it to happen?

> **Theodicy** – literally 'righteous God'. A theodicy is an argument that suggests God is right to allow the existence of evil and suffering because, in some way or another, they are necessary.

> **Typical mistake**
>
> Whenever you are discussing strengths and weaknesses, try to give both sides fairly equal coverage. This will help you to deliver a good, balanced argument.

Irenaean theodicy

Christian theologian St Irenaeus (*c*.125–202 CE) offered a different solution to the problem. In *Against Heresies*, he claimed that, in fact, God deliberately created an imperfect world so that humans could, through trial and adversity, develop into perfect beings. In a sense, evil and suffering are part of God's plans for humanity. In summary, Irenaeus' view was:

- God deliberately created the world and humans imperfectly, in order that they could develop into perfection.

- God created humans with the intention of allowing them to develop.

- God could not have simply created perfect human beings because this would not have given them the chance to choose to be imperfect.

- Perfection had to be developed by humans themselves, and this can be achieved through willing co-operation with God.

- So God had to give humans free will.

- This means God gave humans the right to freely choose either good or evil.

- Therefore God had to permit evil and suffering to occur.

Exam tip

When discussing an argument, do so in logical and progressive steps. This will make your answer much clearer.

British philosopher and theologian John Hick (1922–2012) agreed. In *Philosophy of Religion* (1973) he said that God had to allow humans to develop for themselves. If God had made humans perfect, then they would have had what he called the 'goodness of robots', who would automatically love God without thought. This is not the most loving thing to do. He went on:

- God had to created humans at an **epistemic distance** from himself so that God would not be so close that humans would be overwhelmed by him and have no choice but to believe.

- By keeping at a distance, God allows humans to choose freely.

- The world has to be imperfect because if it were perfect, then there would be no evil and suffering and humans would not be free to choose, because in a perfect world, only good could happen.

- Evil and suffering allow humans to develop positive qualities such as love or courage.

- If God constantly interfered, then humans simply could not develop. This is known as the **counter-factual hypothesis**.

- Hick said that the world is a place where humans have to face challenges in order to gain perfection. He said that the world is: 'rather well adapted to the quite different purpose of "soul making"'.

Epistemic distance – God keeps a distance from humanity in order not to overwhelm.

Counter-factual hypothesis – If God interferes, then humanity cannot develop.

Criticisms of the Irenaean theodicy

There are a number of criticisms against Irenaeus:

- Suffering does not always result in positive human development.
- Suffering can produce nothing but misery and suffering.
- Why are there such extremes of suffering and do such happenings really produce good?
- British theologian D. Z. Phillips (1934–2006) argued in *The Concept of Prayer* (1976) that love can never be expressed by allowing suffering to happen.

Key quote

'What are we to say of the child dying from cancer? If this has been "done" to anyone that is bad enough, but to be done for a purpose planned from eternity — that is the deepest evil. If God is this kind of agent, He cannot justify His actions and His evil nature is revealed.'

(D. Z. Phillips)

Now test yourself

Tested ☐

4 What does 'theodicy' mean?

5 According to Augustus, where did evil come from?

6 Who spoke about the 'goodness of robots'?

Answers on page 61

Exam tip

Don't forget that this is a Religious Studies examination so it is always a good idea to use quotations from the Bible or other sacred texts to support your answer. Try this: The argument Hick makes agrees with the biblical teaching of St Paul:

'We rejoice in our sufferings because we know that suffering produces perseverance, perseverance, character, and character, hope.'

(Romans 5:3)

The free will defence

Revised ☐

A modern answer to the problem of evil and suffering has become known as the 'free will defence'. Swinburne explained it as follows:

- This world is the logically necessary environment for humans to develop.
- It provides freedom to make choices, both good and evil.
- Without such choices, people would not be free.
- God cannot intervene because to do so would interfere with human freedom.
- 'The less he allows men to bring about large-scale horrors, the less freedom and responsibility he gives them' (Swinburne, *The Existence of God*).
- People must take our responsibilities seriously. Swinburne: 'If there is always another chance there is no risk.'
- The world has natural laws that can cause suffering. Swinburne: 'If men are to have knowledge of the evil which will result from their actions or negligence, laws of nature must operate regularly: and that means that there will be victims of the system.'

Exam tip

Try to use scholarly views when discussing why an argument is strong or weak. It will add authority to your answer and show that you have considered the issues carefully.

Criticisms of the free will defence

The main criticism against the free will defence is that it does not sound like the plan of an all-loving God. In *Evil and Omnipotence* (1955), Australian philosopher J. L. Mackie (1917–1981) argued that God could have done better:

'There was open to him [God] the obviously better possibility of making beings who would act freely but always go right. Clearly, his failure to avail himself of this possibility is inconsistent with his being both omnipotent and wholly good.'

An alternative view – Monism

A recent alternative view of the problem is Monism. Monists believe that the universe is good and that evil and suffering are just an illusion of the mind. They argue that:

● We feel suffering only because we cannot see the whole picture.

● This is the best of all words because it was made by an all-loving God. Evil must be an illusion because it cannot be real in such a world.

However, critics of Monism dismiss it because:

● There is real evil and suffering.

● It does not explain why a loving God would allow humanity to suffer from an illusion.

● If evil is only an illusion, why should we bother to try to be good?

● If we were doing evil, then how would we know anyway, since it is an illusion?

Typical mistake

Students tend to stick to traditional arguments. Try something new like Monism – it shows you have 'read around' the subject.

Exam tip

Some students find it difficult to decide how to select a good quotation. The best way is to use good, sharp quotations to illustrate your point, such as this:

'I cannot imagine any omnipotent sentient being sufficiently cruel to create the world we inhabit.'

(the writer and philosopher Iris Murdoch, *A Severed Head*, 1961)

Process theodicy

A rather different answer to the problem of evil and suffering is offered by American philosopher D. R. Griffin (b. 1939) in *God, Power and Evil: A Process Theodicy* (1976). He claimed that:

● The universe is all about continuous creativity – new things happen all the time as part of the universal process and from one thing comes another in a never-ending cycle.

● Sometimes, the process produces good and sometimes evil.

● Even God is developing and changing.

● God is partly distinct and partly part of the universe.

● God can feel the effects of evil and suffering because he is part of the universe. British philosopher A. N. Whitehead (1861–1947) described God as the: '… fellow sufferer who understands'.

● God started off the evolutionary process, which, eventually, led to the development of humans.

● God does not have total control and humans are free to ignore him. Griffin observed: 'God does not refrain from controlling the creatures simply because it is better for God to use persuasion, but because it is necessarily the case that God cannot completely control the creatures.'

Criticisms of process theodicy

Process theodicy has many weaknesses:

- It denies that God is all-powerful.
- God is not all-loving.
- God seems to allow suffering and wrong doing.
- Is this God a being worthy of worship?
- Does good outweigh evil?

Hick argued:

'The God of process theodicy is ... the God of the elite, or the great and successful among humankind ... This is not the God of those millions who have been crippled by malnutrition and have suffered and died under oppression and exploitation, plague and famine, flood and earthquake ...'

Now test yourself

7 What is an 'epistemic distance'?

8 Why did Hick say that evil and suffering could be 'soul making'?

9 What did Whitehead mean when he called God 'a fellow sufferer who understands'?

Answers on page 61

Tested

Conclusion

It may be that there is no God and evil and suffering are simply part of human existence. Yet evil and suffering also offer the possibility that they are, indeed, a part of God's plan for humanity.

Key quote

'A generous God will seek to give us great responsibility for ourselves, each other, and the world, and thus a share in his own creative activity of determining what sort of world it is to be. And he will seek to make our lives valuable, of great use to ourselves and to each other. The problem is that God cannot give us these goods in full measure without allowing much evil on the way.'

(Richard Swinburne)

Summary

- Evil and suffering are a major argument against the existence of God.
- Inconsistent triad – God is all-powerful and all-loving, but appears not to stop evil and suffering.
- Suffering may be a punishment/illusion or test of faith.
- Suffering comes from original sin and humanity's rejection of God (Biblical view).
- Evil comes from rejection of God (Augustinian theodicy).
- Suffering enables humanity to grow and develop (Irenaeus).
- God cannot interfere because he gave humans free will (Swinburne).
- God is part of universal process and cannot stop evil (Process theodicy).

Exam practice

(a) Examine any two possible answers to the problem of evil and suffering.

(b) To what extent is the problem of evil and suffering impossible to resolve?

Answer guidance online

Online

2.2 Miracles

Key ideas

Miracles, if they exist, are convincing proof of the existence of God. But what is a miracle? Scholars have offered various views:

- 'A miracle occurs when the world is not left to itself, when something distinct from the natural order as a whole intrudes into it.' (Mackie, *The Miracle of Theism*, 1982).

- 'It is possible to define the term in either purely physical and non-religious terms, as a breach or suspension of natural law, or in religious terms, as an unusual and striking event that evokes and mediates a vivid awareness of God.' (Hick, *Philosophy of Religion*, 1990).

- '... an event which is astonishing, unusual, shaking, without contradicting the rational structure of reality ... an event which points to the mystery of being.' (Tillich, *Systematic Theology*, 1953).

To be a miracle, an act must:

- break a natural law
- have a clear purpose and significance
- be best explained as an act of God.

Exam tip

Don't box yourself into a corner by saying that an event has to be a violation of a natural law in order to fulfil the definition of 'miracle'. You can generate a wider range of discussion by considering the range of possible interpretations.

Typical mistake

When talking about miracles, try to avoid the assumption that all miracles involve the breaking of a natural law and are therefore physically impossible. Again, you will be limited in how you can respond to a question if you do this.

The view of St Thomas Aquinas   Revised ☐

Thomas Aquinas referred to miracles as 'those things ... which are done by divine power apart from the order generally followed in things'. He said that God was **interventionalist**, in that, through miracles, he involves himself in human affairs. Aquinas said that there were three types of miracle:

- Events done by God, which nature could never do, for example, stopping the sun (Joshua 10:13). These are strong miracles – events which are considered to be impossible, for example, the raising from the dead of a person who had been clinically dead for more than 24 hours would be such an event.

- Events done by God, which nature could do, but not in that order, for example, exorcisms (Mark 1:31). These events would not be inconceivable, but certainly highly unexpected. They are not technically impossible and may include many modern accounts of healings from terminal illnesses.

- Events done by God, which nature can do, but God does without the use of **natural laws**, for example, the healing of Peter's mother-in-law (Mark 1:29–31). These events are not physically impossible. These are weak miracles since there is little proof that the event is out of the ordinary.

Interventionalist – God, through miracles, intervenes in human affairs.

Natural laws – the laws of nature, upon which science is based, that govern the way the universe seems to operate.

Exam tip

A major criticism of Aquinas' viewpoint is based on the idea that God breaks natural laws. The problem is that we may not know all natural laws, nor how they operate. We cannot, therefore, tell if a natural law has been broken or not.

Other views on miracles

Revised

Coincidences

Sometimes people believe that an astonishing coincidence is a miracle. R. F. Holland called those events which constitute a 'coincidence … taken religiously as a sign and called a miracle' (*Religion and Understanding*, 1967). Events of this kind do not really qualify as miracles because they do not involve natural events or laws, but are beneficial coincidences. Holland typically uses the example of the boy trapped on the railway track, saved when the train unexpectedly stops before the inevitable and fatal collision. These miracles are weaker still than Aquinas' third category, since no natural event takes place at all. A non-natural series of events is interpreted as having special significance which points towards God's intervention, but there is no physical, logical or philosophical reason why the event may not have happened without any external influence at work.

Biblical miracles

The Bible interprets all events, including miracles, in terms of the relationship between God and humanity. The miracles of the Bible raise particular problems because their purpose and intention is not obvious. For instance:

- The miracles of Jesus are clearly intended to be signs and not just events to marvel at. They point to who he is and what he teaches about God and they are a response to faith.

- The miracles in the Bible may be myths – that is stories which didn't prove that something was absolutely true, but that reflected reflected a way of thinking about the world which was not intended to be taken literally.

- German theologian Rudolph Bultmann (1884–1976) observed that 'it is impossible to use electric light and the wireless, and to avail ourselves of modern medical and surgical discoveries and at the same time believe in the New Testament world of spirits and demons.'

- He suggested that biblical miracles should be **demythologised**, by focusing on the spiritual truths they revealed rather than worrying about what actually happened.

Exam tip

Remember that the term 'miracle' can have several legitimate meanings, but you should know David Hume's classic definition from *An Enquiry Concerning Human Understanding*: 'The transgression of a law of nature by a particular volition of the Deity, or by the interposition of some invisible agent.'

Exam tip

Make sure that you consider the ways in which different definitions of miracles may make it easier or harder to believe that miracles can occur. Use the views of scholars to support your view.

Demythologise – taking away the fictional stories in the scripture, leaving only the spiritual truths behind.

Reasons to believe in miracles

Richard Swinburne

In *The Concept of Miracle* (1970), Swinburne said that God always acts for a reason and that miracles must have deep religious significance:

> 'If a god intervened in the natural order to make a feather land here rather than there for no deep, ultimate purpose, or to upset a child's box of toys just for spite, these events would not naturally be described as miracles.'

- It is possible that the best explanation for an event is that it is indeed a miracle.
- The evidence in favour of a miracle must be considered properly, not just dismissed because it may not be scientific.
- It is reasonable to adopt principles of testimony and credulity – the assumption that people tell the truth and it is therefore reasonable to believe them.
- Miracles are consistent with the nature of loving God to help humanity.

> **Now test yourself**
>
> 1 What is an 'interventionalist God'?
> 2 What is natural evil?
> 3 What is the principle of testimony?
>
> **Answers on page 61**
>
> Tested

John Locke

In *A Discourse of Miracles* (1974) English philosopher John Locke (1632–1704) argued that true miracles must:

- act as a witness to the existence of God and therefore: 'Miracles must testify to truths relating to the glory of God and the great concern of men.'
- be testified to by a trustworthy messenger from God: '...he who comes with a message from God to be delivered to the world, cannot be refused belief if he vouches his mission by a miracle, because his credentials have a right to it.'

Keith Ward

British philosopher Keith Ward (b. 1938) claimed that God is the 'terminus' (end) of the quest for intelligibility.

- God is a rational complete explanation for events which are otherwise inexplicable.
- There are accounts of miracles that cannot be explained by science or medicine.

> **Now test yourself**
>
> Tested
>
> 4 What is a 'strong' miracle?
> 5 Who wanted to demythologise the Bible?
> 6 Who claimed that miracles were consistent with God's loving nature?
> 7 Who said that miracles were the terminus of the quest for intelligibility?
>
> **Answers on page 61**

> **Exam tip**
>
> Use solid examples, for instance, more than 70 miracle cures at Lourdes have been ratified by the Vatican and thousands more by individuals healed at prayer meetings. This enables you to offer good support to your arguments and illustrate important issues.

Philosophical problems concerning miracles

There are a number of different philosophical problems concerning miracles. The main ones are:

- If there is no God, then how can miracles occur?
- Miracles are just occurrences that we cannot explain at the time but, in the future, science will.
- Testimonies of miraculous occurrences are false or mistaken.
- If God is all-loving and all-powerful, why doesn't he intervene with miracles more often?

Science – Peter Atkins   Revised

Some philosophers argue that there are no such things as miracles and that, one day, science will explain what really happened. British scientist Peter Atkins (b. 1940) wrote:

'Everything in the universe can be explained in terms of physical science.'
(Dialogue, 1998)

He argued that:

- There are no miracles, because we know the laws of nature and they are reliable and unchanging.
- Reports of miracles are simply wrong because they deny this understanding of how the world works.
- Atkins observed: 'God is the last resort of feeble minds masquerading as truth. Science … respects nobility of the human spirit.'

Personhood – Gareth Moore   Revised

In 'Believing in God: A Philosophical Essay' (1988), Catholic philosopher Gareth Moore (1948–2002) argued that:

- God is not a person and therefore cannot perform miracles.
- To claim that God performed a miracle is actually the same as saying that *no one* performed the act.

Exam tip

It will impress the examiner if you can offer more than one scholarly view – for instance, using both Atkins and Moore together. This shows that you have considered both sides of the argument.

The moral dimension – Peter Vardy   Revised

In *The Puzzle of God* (Fount, 1999) British philosopher and theologian Peter Vardy (b. 1945) said that there were good moral reasons for saying that there were no miracles. He argued that:

- There are so many trivial miracles that are reported.
- God fails to act where there is great suffering and a real need for miracles: 'A God who intervenes at Lourdes to cure an old man of cancer but does not act to save starving millions in Ethiopia – such a God needs, at least, to face some hard moral questioning.'
- Certain miracles seem to be incompatible with the notion of love.
- God appears to help some people through miracles, but not others. Why does he not treat everyone equally? This is morally incompatible.

The views of David Hume

Revised

The most influential philosopher concerning miracles is Hume and his essay 'Of Miracles', in *An Enquiry Concerning Human Understanding* (1748). He defined a miracle as:

'A transgression of a law of nature by a particular volition of the Deity.'

He said there were no such things as miracles because:

- There were not enough reliable witnesses: 'There is not to be found in all history, any miracle attested by a sufficient number of men, of such unquestioned good sense, education and learning, as to secure as against all delusion.'
- Only religious believers testified to miracles and they were unreliable because they are always looking for miracles: '... a religionist may be an enthusiast and imagines he sees what has no reality.'
- Miracle stories tended to come from unreliable places: 'It forms a strong presumption against all supernatural and miraculous relations that they are observed chiefly to abound amongst ignorant and barbarous nations.'
- Miracles are an important part in many different religions. If all religions reported miracles, then these claims cancelled each other out: '... every miracle, therefore, pretended to have been wrought in any of these religions ... destroys the credit of those miracles.'

Criticisms of Hume

- Hume believed the laws of nature were fixed and therefore could not be violated. However, scientific advances since Hume's time would look to him like a violation of natural law, for example, using aeroplanes to fly across the world.
- Hume's language is very ambiguous. He does not say what 'unquestioned good sense, education and learning' means.
- Hume suggests that only religious believers see miracles and implies that, because of this, their testimonies are unreliable. Yet why should religious believers be more unreliable than anyone else?
- Hume argues that it is not possible for God to work miracles for people in different religions and that the testimonies of miracles from different religions cancel each other out. But why should this be so? If there is a God, he could work to help everyone.

Conclusion

There is no certain answer as to whether or not miracles actually occur – nor is there an agreed definition on what a miracle actually is. For those who have religious faith, miracles are completely consistent with the existence of God.

Key quote

'If there is a God, one might well expect him to make his presence known to man, not merely through the over-all pattern of the universe in which he placed them, but by dealing more intimately and personally with them.'

(Richard Swinburne)

But for those who do not believe in God, then it is impossible for miracles to occur. As Atkins observed:

'There is a sharp contrast between the impenetrable prose of theological comprehension, which is largely pretentious gobbledegook, and the sharp, limpid explanations of science.'

For believers, miracles are the ultimate proof of the existence of God. For non-believers, they are meaningless and impossible. There is no certain answer.

Now test yourself

Tested ☐

8 Why did Vardy suggest that miracles were morally incompatible?
9 Why did Hume reject testimonies of miracles from religious believers?
10 Why did Atkins call miracles 'largely pretentious gobbledegook'?

Answers on page 61

Summary

- There are several definitions of a miracle. The most well-known is a breaking of the laws of nature by God for a religious purpose.
- Aquinas' use of strong and weak miracles are useful aids for identifying reliable evidence and testimony of miracles.
- God is interventionalist and uses miracles to affect human life.
- It is useful to compare biblical miracles and modern testimony of miracles e.g. events at Lourdes.
- Arguments in support of miracles from Swinburne, who sees them as logical manifestation of God's love.
- Arguments against from Holland (coincidences) and Vardy (moral grounds).
- Atkins offers the view that science will one day explain miracles.
- Hume's view is that testimonies of miracles are unreliable.

Exam practice

(a) Examine the view that miracles are a convincing proof of the existence of God.

(b) To what extent are the arguments against miracles convincing?

Answer guidance online

Online ☐

1.1 The relationship between Religion and Morality

Key themes

Some believe that religion and morality are similar, if not the same. They claim that moral duties and obligations are actually commands with authority behind them. The issue is: who or what is the source of that authority? Is it God?

Religious believers may argue that part of what it means to believe in God is to follow God's moral commands, such as not stealing, murdering or committing **adultery**.

The problem remains, does all of morality come from God, or from elsewhere? People who are not religious may nevertheless lead good moral lives. Where do they think that morality comes from, if they don't believe in God?

There are three main viewpoints of the relationship between religion and morality:

- Morality depends on religion. Without religion there would be no morality and no way to judge right from wrong. The ultimate source of moral authority is God.
- Morality is independent of religion. Morality comes from cultural and social viewpoints.
- Morality is opposed to religion. Religious teachings are outdated and irrelevant. If there is no God then there can be no religious morality, therefore morality must come from humanity itself.

> **Adultery** – having sex with someone when you are married to someone else.

Typical mistake

Don't just limit your answer here to the Bible. You need also to mention how religious believers for example, give authority to church teaching and doctrine and the teaching of the Pope. You may also refer to other religious traditions.

Supporting arguments

Divine command ethics

Divine command ethics is the view that sacred texts provide moral standards, such as the Ten Commandments found in the Bible (Exodus 20) or the first Surah of the Qur'an which states: 'Guide us along the straight path.'

Divine command ethics argues that:

- God decides what is right and wrong.
- Human reason has no authority.
- God has absolute authority.
- Humans must accept God's teaching.
- God is the only source of moral guidance.
- Those who fail to obey God will be punished.
- Philosopher A. C. Grayling (b. 1949) observes: 'Sin is disobedience to the commands of God; virtue is obedience to them.' (*What is Good?*, 2003).

However, there are problems with this view:

- If humans obey God's moral commands simply because they fear punishment, they are acting out of self-preservation rather than morally.
- German philosopher Immanuel Kant (1724–1804) said that fear of punishment should not be the motivation for moral goodness: 'Morality must not lower herself. Her own nature must be her recommendation. All else, even divine reward, is nothing else beside her …' (*Lectures on Ethics*, ed. 1981).
- If being morally good means doing what God commands, then humans have no choice and no chance to decide what is right or wrong for themselves.
- How can we be sure that what God commands is always morally right?
- Do only those who fully obey God's moral commands get an afterlife?

> **Divine command ethics –** Morality is based on commands given by God.

> **Exam tip**
>
> Remember that sacred texts contain many examples of God's moral commandments, so try to use good ones, such as:
>
> **'You shall not steal'**
> (Exodus 20 v.15)
>
> and
>
> **'Love your neighbour as yourself'** (Luke 10 v.27)
>
> These will be useful to support your arguments.

St Thomas Aquinas

In *Summa Thelogica*, Aquinas supported the view that religion and morality were linked. He said that:

- God is the supreme good: 'Therefore there must also be something which is to all beings the cause of their being, goodness, and every other perfection, and this we call God.' (cited in *The Existence of God*, ed. J. Hick, 1964).
- The goodness found in human beings and in the world is a reflection of the supreme goodness of God.
- God, being perfect in goodness, is also perfect in his very being.
- Catholic philosopher and theologian Frederick Copleston (1907–1994) supported this when he claimed: 'I do think that all goodness reflects God in some way and proceeds from him, so that in a sense the man who loves what is truly good, loves God.' (cited in *The Existence of God*, ed. J. Hick, 1964).

> **Exam tip**
>
> Be careful about the wording – make sure you get the terms used by the philosophers and the names of the sacred texts the right way around!

Immanuel Kant

In 'The Critique of Practical Reason', Kant offered an argument for the existence of God based on the existence of morality. He claimed that:

- The existence of God is the only reason to be moral.
- God is needed if we are to achieve the ultimate aim of morality; the greatest good or '**summum bonum**'.
- All humans have a *duty*, or a **categorical imperative**, to seek the highest form of good – the '*summum bonum*'.
- Moral perfection will never be achieved in this life.
- Humans will need an afterlife to achieve the '*summum bonum*'.
- Therefore, God must exist in order to provide an afterlife and allow humanity to reach moral perfection.
- The existence of God is necessary to achieve the goal of morality.

Exam tip

Remember to make clear in your answer that Kant's proof is an *a priori* proof, known by reason rather than **empirical** observation. This will help you to explain Kant's views more clearly.

Typical mistake

Many students forget that this is a Religious Studies examination. Using scripture and church doctrine can be a great help in developing your answer.

Conscience

Morality may be dependent on religion through the conscience, which some regard as God given, or even the voice of God, which enables people to discern right from wrong according to God's will. Many religious believers support this view of the conscience. For instance, in the Bible, the apostle Paul speaks of the conscience as:

- Something which all humans have as a gift from God (Romans 2:12).
- It enables them to hear God, despite their sinful nature.
- Those who follow their conscience and love God will gain eternal life (Romans 3:21–22).

More recently, in the Roman Catholic Church:

- The Vatican II '*Gaudium et Spes*' document declared: 'Deep within his conscience man discovers a law which he has not laid upon himself but he must obey.'
- Theologian Cardinal J. H. Newman (1801–1890) maintained that the conscience was the means by which we know about the existence and nature of God.

However, having a conscience is not, of itself, quite enough because:

- The conscience needs to be instructed and trained.
- The more right choices people make, the more people will be naturally inclined to make the right choice in the future.
- Conscience needs the aid of natural law to enable people to rationally recognise moral behaviour.
- This will eventually lead humans to an acknowledgement of God's moral law.
- For the believer, training the conscience must involve a continuous attempt to work out God's will.

Summum bonum – the state of ultimate or greatest good.

Categorical imperative – obeying a moral command out of reason or duty.

Empirical – using evidence gained from the senses – touch, smell, sight, taste, sound.

There are strong arguments against associating conscience with the moral teachings of God because:

- Conscience is not the same in everyone.

- It may be simply a human interpretation and therefore could be mistaken.

- Rather than understand conscience as God given, conscience may be part of human make-up to control social behaviour.

Typical mistake

Don't fall into the trap that some examination candidates do of only arguing from one point of view in an evaluation answer. In questions that ask you to evaluate or assess, you will find that you can only do these properly if you can consider both sides of an argument. Only then can you decide which side of the argument is the most convincing.

Now test yourself

Tested

1 What are the three viewpoints concerning the relationship between religion and morality?
2 What is divine command ethics?
3 What is the categorical imperative?
4 What did Kant call the state of ultimate good?
5 What did Paul say that conscience was?

Answers on pages 61–62

Independent concepts

There are many reasons for arguing that religion and morality are independent of each other:

- Moral teaching based on scripture is unreliable because sacred texts are ancient and linked to cultural customs of the past.

- There are problems of interpretation and meaning as a result of translation.

- If religious believers are morally good only in the hope of receiving a reward or avoiding punishment, is this genuine goodness?

- Too much pressure is put on religious believers to live up to unrealistic standards of goodness.

- Society only adheres to religious morality in times of crisis.

- Ancient religious ideas sometimes prevent moral progress.

Exam practice answer guidance at **www.therevisionbutton.co.uk/myrevisionnotes**

The Euthyphro Dilemma

The greatest challenge to the relationship between religion and morality was posed by Plato in the **Euthyphro Dilemma** in *Phaedo*:

'Do the gods love that which is holy, or is it holy because it is loved by the gods?'

What Plato argued was 'Does God command X because it is good, or is X good because God commands it?' There are two possible views:

- Does God command X because it is good? In this case goodness exists as something separate from God.
- Is X good simply because God commands it? In this case, God is the direct source of moral knowledge. God's commands establish what is good, and nothing can be good unless God commands it.

This can cause a real dilemma because if X is good because God commands it, then *anything* God commands must be good. But what happens if what God commands contradicts human morality?

> **Euthyphro Dilemma** – does God command what is good or is it good because God commands it?

> **Typical mistake**
> The Euthyphro Dilemma is a very important concept and can be readily used in examination answers, but many candidates get it wrong or confused. Make sure that you know it properly.

Opposing concepts

Some believe that religion and morality are opposed, in part because of the apparent immoral actions in the sacred texts – for instance the alleged mass killing of humanity by God in the flood of Noah's Ark (Genesis 6–7) or the killing of the firstborn in Egypt (Exodus 12), which point to an immoral God who is not the source of all goodness.

British philosopher R. A. Sharpe (1935–2006) in *The Moral case against Religious Belief* (1997) claimed it is absurd that, in the light of modern developments, ancient religious moral commands have authority today – for instance, the Catholic ban on contraception:

'Is it remotely conceivable that God should be interested in whether people use a condom rather than the rhythm method of contraception?'

Friedrich Nietzsche

German philosopher Nietzsche (1844–1900) supported this view, saying that following religious morals was a slave morality by which suffering and weakness were seen as good. Nietzsche believed that one day, humanity would develop a full code of morality without using the scriptures. He wrote that humanity will:

'… develop his own, independent, long-range will, which dares to make promises; he has a sense of power and freedom, of absolute accomplishment.'
(cited in Habgood, *Varieties of Unbelief*, 2000)

Samuel Porter Putnam also supported this, writing:

'The moment one loses confidence in God or immortality, one becomes more self reliant, more courageous, and the more solicitous to aid where only human aid is possible.'
(*My Religious Experience*, 1981)

Today we live in a multicultural world which is largely **secular**, though religious morality is still present. We are very aware of the diversity of religious traditions and moralities and we can see just how powerfully religious morality can be. Yet for Grayling, religion is irrelevant to contemporary secular morality:

> '... religion is precisely the wrong resource for thinking about moral issues in the contemporary world, and indeed subverts moral debate.'

> (*What is Good?*, 2003)

> **Secular** – belonging to the world, rather than religion.

Exam tip

It is helpful in examination answers to add extra relevant detail. For instance, here you could add that Grayling suggests modern society values freedom, achievement, saving money, insuring against the future and being rewarded for success, while Christian morality in particular values the opposite: 'It tells people to take no thought for tomorrow, to give their possessions to the poor, and to be aware that a well off person will find heaven unwelcoming.'

Now test yourself   Tested ☐

6 What is the Euthyphro Dilemma?
7 What was the basis of R. A. Sharpe's criticisms?
8 Who called religious morality a 'slave morality'?
9 Who said 'the man who loves what is truly good, loves God?'

Answers on page 62

Conclusion

It seems that religion has certainly made a significant contribution to human morality and, in that respect, deserves a great deal of credit, whether or not those moral commands actually come from God.

Yet many questions still remain. For instance, how would a religious and a non-religious person respond to these statements?

- Sacred texts should be obeyed without question.
- Humans should be free from religious influence and make their own moral codes.
- Religious morality holds back human development.
- Religious morality is the only hope for the future.

Summary

✔ Scholars accept that religion and morality are similar, but not the same.

✔ The dilemma concerns whether or not morality comes from God.

✔ Divine Command Ethics suggests morality comes from God through the scripture.

✔ Aquinas and others suggest we know God's moral commands through conscience.

✔ Others argue that conscience is not the same in everyone, so how can it come from God?

✔ Plato's Euthyphro Dilemma questions God as the source of morality.

✔ Others argue that religious morality is out of date and does not apply in modern times.

✔ Secularists argue morality comes from human reason and need.

Exam practice

(a) Consider the view that religion and morality are linked.

(b) Comment critically on the view that there is no link between religion and morality.

Answer guidance online

Online ☐

1.2 Utilitarianism and Situation Ethics

Key themes: Utilitarianism

Utilitarianism, from the Latin word '*utilis*', meaning useful, is an ethical theory based upon the principle of utility, which says that the right action is the one which produces the greatest happiness for the most people. It is usually summarised as: 'The greatest good for the greatest number.'

It comes from the work of English philosopher and social reformer Jeremy Bentham (1748–1832), who wrote in *An Introduction to the Principles of Morals and Legislation*:

> 'By utility is meant that property of any object whereby it tends to produce benefit, advantage, pleasure, good or happiness or to prevent the happening of mischief, pain, evil or unhappiness.'

Utilitarianism is:

- A **relativistic moral theory**: there are no absolute moral rules that everyone must obey.
- A **teleological theory**: moral truth can be found through nature and purpose.
- A **consequentialist theory**: the right thing to do depends upon the consequence of actions.

Relativistic moral theory – where there are no absolute moral rules.

Teleological theory – truth is discovered through nature and purpose.

Consequentialist theory – the right thing depends on the consequences and end result.

Hedonic Calculus – involves calculating the amount of pleasure by considering seven key factors about the practical application of pleasure.

Jeremy Bentham and Act Utilitarianism
Revised

Bentham proposed 'Act Utilitarianism' which stated that it would be possible to judge the good or evil in a particular action according to the consequences of the action.

Bentham devised the **Hedonic Calculus** to calculate the most pleasurable actions. He suggested that:

- Good or bad actions can be worked out according to predicted results.
- We can calculate which action is more likely to produce the right result by reaching a happiness score.
- The aim is to measure the moral value of an act by reference to the consequences.
- It measures by the *quantity* of the pain or happiness.

Exam tip

You must emphasise the point that Bentham's theory is one of **universal ethical hedonism**; everyone is equal and has an equal right to happiness. If an action increases pleasure, then it is right and what is right for society is that which provides the greatest happiness of the majority. This will be a crucial aspect of any Utilitarianism question.

Universal ethical hedonism – everyone has an equal right to happiness.

The Hedonic Calculus offers seven elements:

- Intensity – is the happiness or pain deep or superficial?
- Duration – is it temporary or permanent?
- Certainty – how sure is it that the act will lead to happiness or pain?
- Propinquity (remoteness) – does the act create happiness/pain for people close to us?
- Fecundity (richness) – does the pain/happiness make things better or worse?
- Purity – is the act morally pure?
- Extent of pleasure – does the happiness/pain touch the whole life of a person, or just part?

Criticisms of the Hedonic Calculus

In *The Puzzle of Ethics*, modern philosophers Peter Vardy and Paul Grosch criticised the calculus for three reasons:

- It measures happiness in terms of quantity rather than quality.
- It is dependent on being able to accurately predict the consequences of any act.
- It is difficult to say what counts as happiness or pain.

> **Typical mistake**
>
> You don't need to learn the Calculus elements in order by heart – you just need to know how they are applied in making a moral decision.

John Stuart Mill and Rule Utilitarianism

Revised

English philosopher and economist, John Stuart Mill (1806–1873), in *Utilitarianism: Essays on Ethics*, criticised Bentham's act utilitarianism because he thought that:

- It justified what he saw as lower pleasures, such as violence if the action was justified by the majority.
- It was possible to educate people to seek higher pleasures.
- He spoke up for 'Rule Utilitarianism', which starts by defining what is morally right by considering the consequences of acting in accordance with rules.

Mill believed that morality should be:

- based on what is good – truth, beauty, love and friendship
- based on higher pleasures because they have greater moral worth
- based on certain rules that promote happiness, such as keeping promises or not stealing
- about following established rules and considering the practical consequences of an action before carrying it out.

Mill proposed the 'harm principle' which suggested that:

- The majority can only pressure the minority if it prevents harm.
- Not all pleasures are equal.
- Pleasures of the mind are superior physical pleasures.
- He famously observed: 'It is better to be a human being dissatisfied than a pig satisfied; better to be Socrates dissatisfied than a fool satisfied.'

> **Exam tip**
>
> This is a crucial concept. Mill distinguished between 'higher pleasures' of the mind (such as reading books) and 'lower pleasures' of the physical body (such as getting drunk). He believed that once certain lower pleasures (e.g. food, shelter and warmth) had been satisfied, then people should move on to higher pleasures – intellectual, cultural and spiritual. He wrote:
>
> '… people lose their high aspirations as they lose their intellectual tastes, because they have no time or opportunity for indulging them; and they addict themselves to inferior pleasures.'

> **Exam tip**
>
> Make sure you understand the difference between Bentham and Mill. Bentham refers to quantitative pleasure while Mill talks about qualitative pleasure.

Criticisms of Mill

The main criticisms of Mill's view are:

- It may be very difficult to distinguish between higher and lower pleasures.
- It is not possible to rely on one moral principle, namely the greatest happiness for the greatest number, to solve all moral problems.

Now test yourself

1 What is 'act utilitarianism'?
2 What is 'rule utilitarianism'?
3 What does 'propinquity' mean?
4 What is 'fecundity'?
5 What is the 'harm principle'?

Answers on page 62

Tested

Modern views

Strengths and weaknesses of Utilitarianism

Revised

Preference Utilitarianism is a theory developed by British moral philosopher R. M. Hare (1919–2002). It suggests that, when deciding what the right thing is to do, then 'pleasure' should be replaced by 'best interests'. In *Essays in Ethical Theory* (1989), Hare said that the preferences of individuals should always be taken into account and that the right thing to do is to maximise the chances of everyone's preferences being satisfied.

Negative Utilitarianism is a view developed by philosopher Karl Popper (1902–1994), who suggested that the right thing to do is to promote the least evil or harm or, in other words, to reduce the amount of suffering for the greatest number.

The strength of both viewpoints is that they offer a better chance for everyone to be happy in given circumstances. However, their weakness lies in the fact that it is almost impossible to predict and foresee all the possible consequences of a given action.

Strengths of Utilitarianism	Weaknesses of Utilitarianism
It supports the view that human well-being is good.	It requires people to predict the long-term consequences of an action.
Actions should be judged according to their effect on this well-being.	There is no guarantee that circumstances will turn out exactly as predicted.
A person's motives may be good or bad, but only consequences matter.	Not every action done out of good will is going to result in good consequences.
It encourages democracy and the interests of the majority.	Happiness changes from one person to another.
Circumstances can be judged without reference to previous ones.	It does not allow for someone doing what they believe to be morally right whatever the consequences.
It does not rely on religious principles.	The theory cannot be used to decide what is truly good.
	The majority is not always right.
	The theory can lead to injustice, particularly on the minority.
	It makes no allowance for personal relationships.
	People may not be motivated by pleasure and happiness.

Now test yourself

Tested

6 Give an example of a 'low pleasure'.
7 Give an example of a 'high pleasure'.
8 Who said: 'Better to be Socrates dissatisfied that a pig satisfied'?

Answers on page 62

Key themes: Situation Ethics

'There is only one ultimate and invariable duty, and its formula is "Thou shalt love thy neighbour as thyself." How to do this is another question, but this is the whole of moral duty.'

(Archbishop William Temple)

Situation Ethics is:

- A relativistic theory. It has no absolute moral rules that have to be followed in every circumstance.
- A consequentialist theory, where the end result is held to be of great importance.
- A teleological theory, claiming that moral truth can be found through nature and purpose.

American philosopher Joseph Fletcher (1905–1991) wrote in *Situation Ethics* (1966) that there are no ethical standards that can be rigidly and consistently applied in all circumstances, since each situation is unique. Ethical theories should be flexible enough to deal with varying circumstances. He wrote: 'For the situationist there are no rules – none at all.'

The features of Fletcher's Situation Ethics are:

- An ethical theory based on the single principle of love.
- People should enter every situation prepared to act in the most loving way.
- The right thing to do in any given situation is the most loving thing to do.

Typical mistake

Make sure that you understand the main differences between Situation Ethics and Utilitarianism. Many students get the two concepts mixed up. Be careful!

The importance of love

Revised

Fletcher defined love in the following way:

- It is always good.
- Love and justice are the same, for love is justice distributed.
- The end result of love justifies the means.
- It makes a decision which is unique to each individual situation.

Typical mistake

Many candidates don't realise that the basis for Fletcher's definition of love is the Greek term *'agape'*, which, in the Bible, refers to God's love for humanity and reflects the kind of love people should have for each other. Jesus said:

'You shall love ... your neighbour as yourself'.

(Luke 10:27)

This could turn out to be a very important part of your answer.

Agape – God's love for humanity.

Every detail can help. For example, here you could make the useful point that Fletcher knew love is very difficult to define. He took the view of love outlined in the Bible by St Paul, who wrote:

'Love is patient, love is kind; love is not envious or boastful or arrogant or rude. It does not insist on its own way; it is not irritable or resentful; it does not rejoice in wrongdoing, but rejoices in the truth. It bears all things, believes all things, hopes all things, endures all things.'

(1 Corinthians 13:4–7)

Now test yourself | Tested ☐

9   Who wrote *Situation Ethics*?
10   What principle is the basis for situation ethics?
11   Who said 'Love is patient, love is kind'?

Answers on page 64

The Four Principles — Revised ☐

In *The Puzzle of Ethics*, Vardy and Grosch highlighted the four principles of Situation Ethics as:

- **Pragmatism**: a proposed course of action, done out of love, should be practical and work in real life.
- **Relativism**: rejects such absolutes as 'never' or 'always'. All situations are individual and unique.
- **Positivism**: decisions should always be made using love as the most important consideration of all.
- **Personalism**: people should always be put first.

Strengths and weaknesses of Situation Ethics — Revised ☐

Strengths of Situation Ethics	Weaknesses of Situation Ethics
• It is easy to understand.	• The absolute law of love is still a law.
• It gives people the freedom to act according to the circumstances.	• It is ambiguous – no two people may agree on what the most loving thing to do actually is.
• It enables people to respond emotionally and/or rationally to the situation, rather than act according to rules.	• It breaks down complex moral situations into individual moral decisions. This may not be the best way to resolve the problem.
• It is based on love.	• It depends too much on an individual's viewpoint.
• Love always seeks the well-being of others.	• It may not be possible to accurately guess the consequences.
	• Are only short-term consequences considered? How do we guess long-term consequences?
	• The theory could justify murder in the interests of love.
	• Does love always justify the suffering of others?
	• Are some types of love better than others?
	• How do we measure love?

Now test yourself | Tested ☐

12   In what sense is situation ethics a relativistic theory?
13   What did Vardy mean when he spoke about 'personalism'?

Answers on page 62

Conclusion

Situation Ethics is controversial. In support, British theologian J. A. T. Robinson (1919–1983) in *Honest to God* said that love was always the best course of action.

> 'Dr Fletcher's approach is the only ethic for 'man come of age'. To resist his approach in the name of religion will not stop it, it will only ensure the form it takes will be anti-Christian.'

Against this, philosopher Graham Dunstan in *Does it matter?*, wrote of Fletcher's theory:

> 'It is possible, though not easy, to forgive Professor Fletcher for writing this book, for he is a generous and loveable man. It is harder to forgive the SCM Press for publishing it.'

Summary

- ✔ Utilitarianism is an ethical theory based on the greatest happiness.
- ✔ It claims there are no moral absolutes and moral solutions are flexible to meet individual situations.
- ✔ Recent versions include preference utilitarianism and negative utilitarianism.
- ✔ Utilitarianism is criticised for being simplistic and unfair.

- ✔ Situation Ethics is based on making decisions through love.
- ✔ It is biblically based and supported.
- ✔ It is reflected in nature and purpose.
- ✔ It is criticised for being simplistic and making it difficult to predict the outcome.

Exam practice

(a) Examine the main principles of Utilitarianism or Situation Ethics.

(b) To what extent is either Utilitarianism or Situation Ethics a convincing ethical theory?

Answer guidance online

Online

2.1 War and peace

Key themes

War and peace play a crucial part in human history and development and cause one of the greatest dilemmas, namely when, if ever, is it right to go to war?

Certainly, Jesus Christ was opposed to war:

'Put your sword back into its place; for all who take the sword will perish by the sword.'

(Matthew 26:52)

Wars happen all over the world for a number of reasons. The main factors of war are:

- selfishness and greed
- rivalry over land
- need for resources and wealth
- national pride
- long-standing hatreds and grievances.

Usually, both sides in a war believe that they have the moral right on their side and both sides tend to misunderstand the other side's point of view. There are several different theories about the main causes of war and civil conflict.

- **Economic**: wars begin as disputes over territory and the natural resources needed for wealth and security.
- **Marxist**: wars are caused by demand for resources.
- **Behaviour**: human beings are naturally violent and transfer their aggression into hatred against their enemies.
- **Leadership**: wars are started not by nations, but by individual leaders such as Hitler who use conflict to maintain their power.
- **Grievances Theory**: wars are caused by religious or ethnic hatreds.

> **Exam tip**
>
> It is useful to give examples of wars and how they began – ask yourself which of the above theories do they fit? This will help you to write a more balanced answer.

The 'Just War'

In Christianity, the issue of whether or not a believer should fight in war has been a difficult dilemma to resolve since Jesus, in particular, told his followers not to fight. It has seemingly been impossible to avoid wars over the centuries, so the Christian Church sought to resolve the dilemma by means of the **Just War** theory, which, formulated by early Christian scholar St Augustine (354–430 CE) and refined by Catholic theologian Thomas Aquinas, allows Christians to fight in wars under certain conditions:

> **Just War** – a war which religious believers may fight in under certain conditions.

Resort to war: *jus ad bellum*

- War must be fought for a just cause: to save life or protect human rights and justice. It is always defensive, never aggressive.
- War must be declared by a competent authority: the government or other legitimate authority.
- There must be comparison of justice on both sides.
- There must be right intention: not undertaken in a spirit of hatred or revenge.
- It must be a last resort, after all efforts at peace have failed.
- There should be a reasonable likelihood of success.

Jus ad bellum – resort to war.

Conduct in war: *jus in bello*

- There should be a reasonable proportion between the injustice being fought and the suffering inflicted by war.
- Proportionality: the use of weapons must be proportional to the threat and only minimum force should be used.
- Warfare must be discriminate: the intentional killing of civilians is always wrong.

Exam tip

Remember that these aspects are crucial to understanding the 'Just War' theory. Make sure that you know them really well.

Jus in bello – conduct in war.

Criticisms of the Just War Theory

Modern warfare has changed the situation considerably since the time of Aquinas and many argue that the Just War theory is no longer applicable because:

- Modern weapons are capable of destroying the whole world.
- Many nations have access to nuclear weapons.
- The war against terrorism is not one nation against another, but one cause against another. Who, in this case, would be the legitimate authority?
- The short- and long-term effects of a nuclear war are impossible to predict.

Moral arguments against the Just War Theory Revised

- War is unjust and all deliberate acts of killing are wrong.
- Morality must oppose violence.
- Just War makes some violence acceptable.
- If the cause is just, then no restrictions should be put upon it.
- Terrorists do not follow Just War principles.

Holy War Revised

A Holy War is one caused by religious differences. It can involve:

- One country with a religion against another with a different religion.
- A religiously motivated group attempting to spread its faith by violence.
- The suppression of one group by another because of its religious practices.

A Holy War has religion at its centre and a belief that God is involved. There are three elements:

- The achievement of a religious goal.
- It must be authorised by a religious leader or the Church.
- A spiritual reward (Heaven) from God for those who take part.

Exam practice answer guidance at **www.therevisionbutton.co.uk/myrevisionnotes**

There are five causes for a Holy War:

- To spread the faith.
- To restore the faith in countries that once belonged to it.
- To rescue believers from unbelieving countries.
- To recover sacred places that have been captured by non-believers.
- To get revenge against those who have committed blasphemies.

Exam tip

Offer real-life past and present examples. These will help to balance and give depth to your answer. For example:

The most famous of the Holy Wars were the Crusades, where Christian armies went to Jerusalem to recover the Christian sacred places from the Muslims. Pope Urban II said at the start of the First Crusade in 1095:

'Let this be your war-cry because this word is given to you by God. When an armed attack is made upon the enemy, let this one cry be raised by all the soldiers of God; it is the will of God ...'

Christianity and 'Holy War' — Revised

The Bible teaches that Holy War is:

- Not against other people or faiths, but against the spiritual forces of evil.
- St Paul wrote: '... take up the shield of faith, with which you can extinguish all the flaming arrows of the evil one. Take the helmet of salvation and the sword of the Spirit, which is the word of God' (Ephesians 5:16–17).
- According to the Bible, this Holy War will culminate in the great final, cosmic, spiritual battle at the end of time.
- It will be won by the Messiah and the angelic armies of heaven.

Islam and the 'Holy War' — Revised

In Islam, Holy War is called **jihad**:

- The **inner jihad** is concerned with a personal spiritual battle within the individual to overcome the forces of evil which prevent them from being close to God. The Qur'an says: 'Those who believe, who strive in the cause of God with their wealth and their persons, are the ones who are successful.'
- The **outer jihad** allows Muslims to fight in order to fight oppression, establish justice and self-defence.

Jihad – holy war in Islam.
Inner jihad – a personal spiritual battle.
Outer jihad – where Muslims fight against oppression.

The outer jihad has strict rules similar to those of the 'Just War', namely:

- It must be authorised by a religious leader.
- It must aim to bring about peace.
- It must be a last resort.
- Innocent civilians must not be targeted.
- Enemies must be treated with justice.

Criticisms of the 'outer jihad'
Revised

- Within Islam, much uncertainty exists about the nature of Holy War.
- There are texts which seem to support the use of violence and war. 'If anyone desires a religion other than Islam it will never be accepted of him' (Surah 3:85).
- Some terrorist acts have been apparently carried out as part of the outer jihad. The prayer of Mohamed Atta shortly before flying an aircraft into the World Trade Center on 11 September 2001 declared: 'God I lay myself in your hands. I ask with the light of your faith that has lit the whole world and lightened all darkness on this earth, to guide me ...'

Nuclear weapons
Revised

Nuclear weapons and weapons of mass destruction (WMDs), such as chemical and biological weapons, have the potential to kill millions and raise special problems for the 'Just War' scenario.

In support of nuclear weapons and WMDs:

- They act as the ultimate deterrent and an enemy will not attack a country which has nuclear weapons or WMDs for fear of being destroyed themselves.
- The existence of such weapons has ensured that there has not been another major world war.

Opposed to nuclear weapons and WMDs:

- They exceed all the terms of a Just War.
- They can cause the loss of millions of innocent lives.
- They can cause great destruction in the hands of terrorists.

> **Exam tip**
>
> Quotations are always useful, especially to break up a series of lengthy paragraphs or bullet points. Remember that all quotations should be relevant and add depth to your answer.

> **Key quotes**
>
> 'Any act of war aimed indiscriminately at the destruction of entire cities or of extensive areas along with their population is a crime against God and man himself.'
>
> (The Second Vatican Council)
>
> 'Such weapons cannot be used without harming non-combatants and could never be proportionate to the just cause and the aim of war.'
>
> (The Church of England's report, 'The Church and the Bomb')

> **Now test yourself**
> Tested
>
> 1 Who said: 'All who take up the sword will perish by the sword'?
> 2 What is the economic theory of conflict?
> 3 What constitutes a competent authority?
> 4 Why is nuclear war incompatible with the 'Just War' theory?
>
> Answers on page 62

Pacifism

In the West, the pacifist movement opposes war, basing its views on the words of Jesus Christ: 'Love your enemies and pray for those who persecute you' (Matthew 5:44).

The principles of pacifism came from the co-founder of the Swiss Brethren Conrad Grebel (1498–1526) who, in 1524, observed:

'The Gospel and those who accept it are not to be protected with the sword, neither should they thus protect themselves.'

There are different types of pacifism:

- Absolute or total pacifism – there should be no use of military force at all, whether or not the cause is just.
- Relative, selective, or conditional pacifism – there may be some circumstances where war might be less bad than the alternative.
- Selective/nuclear pacifism – opposition to nuclear war or the use of weapons of mass destruction.

Key quote

British scholar John Stott (1926–2011) in 'Issues Facing Christians Today' (1990) highlighted the moral dilemma:

'… we must not glamorize or glorify war in itself … in some circumstances it may be defended as the lesser of two evils, but it could never be regarded by the Christian mind as more than a painful necessity in a fallen world.'

A special type of pacifism – non-violence

This type of pacifism was used by Indian leader and peace campaigner Mahatma Gandhi (1869–1948) to persuade enemies to settle disputes peacefully. Techniques of non-violent protest include:

- peaceful demonstrations
- holding vigils
- fasting and hunger strikes
- blockades
- peaceful disobedience.

'It admits no violence under any circumstances whatsoever; and it always insists upon truth.'

(Gandhi)

Criticism of pacifism

- Pacifists could lead to an acceptance of tyranny and oppression.
- Pacifists ought to fight against evil.
- Pacifism leaves a country vulnerable to enemy attack.
- Governments have a duty to protect their citizens.

Typical mistake

You may find that you have strong personal feelings about this topic. Be careful in the examination not to let your own views dominate or distort your answer. Always aim to be objective.

Exam tip

A little background information can add depth to an answer. For instance, here you might include the fact that pacifism came to prominence in the First World War when those pacifists who refused to fight were known as conscientious objectors. Many of these took on non-fighting roles in the armed forces, for example as medical personnel.

Conflict between the positions

There is no doubt that the question of whether or not a religious believer should go to war is a difficult one as religious viewpoints often differ from non-religious ones. Taking Christianity as an example, the New Testament tells believers that:

● Jesus refused to use military power: 'Put your sword back into its place; for all who take the sword will perish by the sword' (Matthew 26:52).

● Jesus taught ideals of righteousness and peace, to love enemies and resist revenge: 'Love your enemies, do good to those that hate you' (Luke 6:27).

● Jesus' opposition to violence, however, was not against the prevention of wrong, or protection of those in need, but against personal insult and threat: 'Do not resist an evil person. If someone strokes you on the right cheek, turn to him your other also' (Matthew 5:39).

● Paul told believers: 'Do not be overcome by evil, but overcome evil with good' (Romans 12:21).

However, in recent times, difficult moral dilemmas have been raised to challenge the Christian viewpoint. For instance:

● Should foreign military forces be used to impose change in places such as Afghanistan?

● Should military force be used to protect innocent families and children, for example, during the genocides in Rwanda and the Balkans?

● Is there such a thing as a 'war on terrorism'?

● In an article 'Just War – War Against Iraq' (2002) philosopher Peter Vardy notes: 'One person's terrorist is another person's freedom fighter and deciding on justice is not easy.'

● Do nations have a moral obligation to protect their citizens?

● Is it right to manufacture and sell weapons?

● Is it right to bomb water or electricity supplies?

● Does pacifism work in the face of extreme evil?

So what is the religious believer to do? John Stott in *Issues Facing Christians Today* said that Christians should 'pray, set an example as "a community of peace", promote public debate on issues of peace and war and believe with confidence that peace is a realistic goal'.

> 'As much as anything, they [Christians] are to live at peace with all, preach the good news of personal salvation, love their enemies, overcome evil with good, deeply respect God's creation and become ministers of reconciliation.'

Exam practice answer guidance at **www.therevisionbutton.co.uk/myrevisionnotes**

Conclusion

Look at the statements below and ask yourself how would a religious believer respond? How would a non-religious believer respond?

- 'War is only right when it is in self-defence.'
- 'War should be the last resort.'
- 'War should be avoided unless our country is directly threatened.'
- 'Sometimes war is necessary to stop people doing bad things.'
- 'Terrorism means that war is necessary.'
- 'War is too expensive to justify.'
- 'We should not go to war to interfere with what is happening in other countries.'
- 'War is needed to help free innocent people.'
- 'War is never right.'
- 'All religious believers should be pacifists.'

The ethics of war and peace play an important role in our lives today. While it is the duty of the state to protect its people, the Just War principles are increasing difficult to apply. Nuclear weapons, weapons of mass destruction and acts of terrorism mean that former ethical standards may have to be re-thought. Perhaps we need a new definition of a Just War?

Now test yourself

5 What is the inner jihad?

6 What is an outer jihad?

7 What does WMD mean?

8 Who first laid out the principles of pacifism?

9 What is a conscientious objector?

10 Which leader is associated with non-violent pacifism and peaceful disobedience?

Answers on page 62

Tested

Summary

- ✔ The dilemma is concerned with if, and when, a religious believer should go to war.
- ✔ The Just War theory allows Christians to fight under certain circumstances.
- ✔ A Holy War is caused by religious beliefs and sometimes supported by scripture.
- ✔ There is a difference between physical and spiritual warfare – the latter is supported by religious belief and teaching.

- ✔ Pacifism is based on religious principle of non-violence.
- ✔ There are many types of pacifism including conditional and nuclear.
- ✔ Pacifism is criticised as being unrealistic and allowing aggressors to thrive.

Exam practice

(a) Examine the conditions under which a Just War may be fought.

(b) To what extent are these conditions effective?

Answer guidance online

Online

2.2 Sexual Ethics

Key themes

Sexual Ethics covers a wide variety of issues and differing attitudes towards:

- marriage
- divorce
- homosexuality
- pornography.

Today, there are widely differing attitudes towards issues relating to sexual ethics and what is, and is not, acceptable sexually. For many people nowadays, sexual pleasure is seen as offering immediate physical pleasure, whilst others believe in the importance of faithfulness, commitment and love in a relationship.

It is a difficult task to define sexual ethics. In *Law, Liberty and Morality* (1986) H. L. Hart concluded that: 'Sexual intercourse between husband and wife is not immoral, but if it takes place in public it is an affront to human decency.'

In the Bible, St Paul makes a similar point:

> **'But if they cannot control themselves, they should marry, for it is better to marry than to burn with passion.'**
>
> (1 Corinthians 7:9)

> **Exam tip**
>
> Sexual ethics is a complex area and you need to use good examples to keep your answer focused. For instance, **adultery** is considered by many people to be immoral, and it provides legal grounds for a divorce, yet it is not a crime.

> **Adultery** – having sex with someone when you are married to someone else

Sex outside marriage

The Christian view — Revised

Many Christians believe that:

- Marriage is the condition that God has established for sexual relationships.
- Sex outside marriage goes against God's will.
- Adultery and homosexuality are also contrary to God's will.
- Love, faithfulness and commitment are important in any sexual relationship.
- Sex is a uniting part of the relationship between husband and wife.

Exam practice answer guidance at **www.therevisionbutton.co.uk/myrevisionnotes**

The libertarian view

The **libertarian view** is that sexual relationships are morally permissible if:

- Both parties are over the legal age limit and consent.
- No harm is done to the other party or to third parties, for example, adultery would not be permitted.
- Consenting adults are free, within these boundaries, to do as they please.

Libertarian view – sexual relationships are morally permissible.

Now test yourself

Tested

1 Who said that it is 'better to marry than burn with passion?'
2 What is the libertarian view?

Answers on page 62

Exam tip

Always remember to consider the weaknesses of an argument. This is important in most examination questions and will add depth to your answer. For example, if there is an imbalance in the relationship then consent is often limited, for instance someone may reluctantly agree to have sex in exchange for money or to get a job.

Utilitarianism and sexuality

Utilitarianism suggests that sexual relations are acceptable as long as:

- They take place in private among consenting adults.
- Nobody else is offended.
- The partners are able to increase their own happiness.

Feminism

Feminists have argued that:

- Religious attitudes to sexual relationships are based on traditional and outdated notions of women as child-raisers and home-makers.
- Sexual behaviour assumes male dominance.
- Women will only be equal when they are free from male sexual dominance.
- Most sex crimes are committed by men.
- Men and women should have equal status in sexual relationships.

Typical mistake

As with the War and Peace unit, don't fall into the trap of getting too involved with your own personal view when writing an answer. Be open-minded and scholarly in your approach.

The internet

It is now possible, with the aid of the internet and online social networks, for people to have intimate relationships (sometimes purely emotional, other times physical – what is known as **cyber sex**), with other people who they never actually meet. This means that:

- People are no longer seen as real individuals, but simply as sexual objects.
- It contradicts the teaching of Jesus: '… everyone who looks at another lustfully has already committed adultery in their heart' (Matthew 5: 28).

Cyber sex – sexual activity through the internet via computers and other technologies.

Marriage and divorce

The Christian view

The Christian view of marriage is that it is:

- ordained by God
- a commitment by a man and woman to a binding relationship that will last until the death of one of the partners.

The purpose of Christian marriage is:

- love, trust and respect for each other (**fidelity**)
- the birth and raising of children (**procreation**).

Some controversies exist however because some Christians believe that:

- there is a natural hierarchy that reflects the relationship of Christ as the groom and the Church as the bride,
- therefore, the husband is the head of the wife and must love and honour her,
- in turn, she must love and respect him: '... each one of you also must love his wife as he loves himself, and the wife must respect her husband' (Ephesians 5:33),
- it can appear there is little equality between the husband and wife: 'Wives, in the same way be submissive to your husband ... Husbands, in the same way be considerate as you live with your wives, and treat them with respect' (1 Peter 3:1,7).

The Christian view of divorce is that:

- The marriage relationship is a holy one and there should be no divorce: '... therefore what God has joined together, let man not separate' (Matthew 19:6).
- Jesus then seems to forbid divorce: 'Anyone who divorces his wife and marries another woman commits adultery. And if she divorces her husband and marries another man, she commits adultery' (Mark 10:11–12).
- However, in Matthew's Gospel, Jesus appears to allow divorce for unfaithfulness: '... anyone who divorces his wife, except for marital unfaithfulness, and marries another woman commits adultery' (Matthew 19:9).
- Some Christians argue that this makes divorce permissible.

> **Fidelity** – love and trust for each other.
>
> **Procreation** – having children.

> **Typical mistake**
>
> Don't fall into the trap of thinking that all Christians oppose divorce. For example, while Roman Catholics are not allowed to divorce, it is permitted in the Church of England, where decisions concerning such matters as whether divorced Christians may marry again will often be left to the individual's conscience or the views of a priest.

> **Now test yourself**
>
> 3 What is the Utilitarian view?
> 4 According to feminism, when will women be equal?
>
> **Answers on page 62**
>
> Tested

Criticism of the Christian view

Critics such as British theologian John Robinson (1919–1983) (See *Honest to God* 1963) argue that the Christian view is wrong because:

- It is out of date.
- It is based on traditional Christian views of human sin and wrongdoing.
- It is based on the absolute command of God.
- It requires people to be more morally good than is possible in real life.
- Jesus' teaching is not clear.

Homosexuality

Homosexuality means having sexual feelings towards members of the same sex, and applies to both men and women. The legal position in the UK today is that:

- Homosexuality is regarded in the same way as heterosexuality.
- Sexual acts are permissible by consenting persons over sixteen and done in private.
- The Civil Partnership Act 2004 allows same-sex couples to register their partnership legally in a civil ceremony. Couples in civil partnerships have the same legal rights as married couples.

Christianity and homosexuality

Revised

Christians are deeply divided over the issue of homosexuality because:

- Homosexual sex cannot lead to reproduction.
- Homosexuality is contrary to the will of God: 'In sacred scripture homosexual acts are condemned as a serious depravity and presented as a sad consequence of rejecting God' (Roman Catholic Church: 'Declaration on Sexual Ethics').

In the 'Catechism of the Catholic Church' (paras. 2357–2359), the Roman Catholic Church teaches that:

- Homosexual people should be treated with respect, compassion and sensitivity.
- Discrimination must be avoided.
- Homosexual feelings are not wrong, but acting on those feelings is.
- Homosexual actions are sinful because they are contrary to God's will because they do not allow for reproduction.
- Homosexuals are encouraged to pray and seek the support of their church to live a life of **chastity**.

> **Chastity** – not having sex for personal reasons

For many Christians from other denominations, homosexuality is sometimes regarded as:

- perfectly natural and the way some people have been created by God
- equal to heterosexuality.

The Church of England acknowledges that the Church must respect those who:

> '... are conscientiously convinced that they have more hope of growing in love for God and neighbour with the help of a loving and faithful homophile partnership, in intention lifelong, where mutual self-giving includes the expression of their attachment.'
>
> (*What the Churches Say*, 2nd edition, 1995)

The Lesbian and Gay Christian Movement 1996 report declares that: 'human sexuality in all its richness is a gift from God gladly to be accepted, enjoyed and honoured'.

In the 1998 Lambeth Conference, the Church of England laid out its view on homosexuality, claiming that there were four possible approaches:

- Homosexuality is a disorder from which the Christian can seek help.
- Homosexual relationships should be **celibate**.
- Committed homosexual relationships are to be preferred over promiscuous ones.
- The Church should fully accept homosexual partnerships and welcome homosexuals into the priesthood.

Celibate – not having sex as a devotion to God.

Controversies

The Christian Church has found it very difficult to resolve moral dilemmas about homosexuality. This is because there are several passages in the Bible that seem to condemn homosexual practices:

- 'If a man lies with a man as one lies with a woman, both of them have done what is detestable. They must be put to death' (Leviticus 20:13).
- 'Do not lie with a man as one lies with a woman; that is detestable' (Leviticus 18:22).
- 'Do not be deceived: Neither the sexually immoral, nor idolaters, nor adulterers, nor male prostitutes nor homosexual offenders … will inherit the kingdom of God' (1 Corinthians 6:9–10).

Exam tip

Remember that this is a Religious Studies examination and that these Biblical quotations are at the very heart of the dilemma so do try to learn them.

There have been controversial incidents in the Church of England when high-ranking clergymen have admitted to being homosexual. For instance:

- In July 2003, following an outcry, Canon Jeffrey John, an openly homosexual though celibate priest, reluctantly withdrew his acceptance of the post of Bishop of Reading.
- This caused great division in the Church. The Dean of Southwark, the Very Reverend Colin Slee, said: 'Canon John has become the victim of appalling prejudice and abuse which has its main proponents within the Church of England … the news will hurt thousands of Christian people who are not gay but believe strongly in God's love and redemption for all his children equally.'
- The Archbishop of Canterbury at the time, Dr Rowan Williams, said: 'This has been a time of open and painful confrontation in which some of our bonds of mutual trust have been severely strained.'

Later in 2003 a split finally happened between the Anglican Churches of the West and the traditional Churches in Nigeria, where homosexuality is illegal and punishable, in some cases, by death. The split occurred when an openly gay priest, Gene Robinson, was ordained as a bishop in the USA. The Nigerian Church, which has 17 million members, openly opposed the ordination and President Olusegun Obasanjo of Nigeria said of homosexuality:

'Such a tendency is clearly un-Biblical, unnatural and definitely un-African.'

Bishop Gene Robinson replied:

'I believe that the acceptance of gay and lesbian people into the life of the church is something that is going to happen … it will happen in God's time.'

Pornography

Pornography is widely available through the media, including the internet and satellite television channels.

The Christian view
Revised

Religious believers oppose pornography for a range of reasons:

- Pornography is often associated with violence.
- It reduces the value and status of human beings as made in the image of God.
- It is an insult to human dignity.
- It involves and encourages addiction and crime.
- It encourages the subordination of women.
- It challenges the loving sexual relationship between husband and wife.

Christians believe that physical life is a gift from God, to be looked after and respected.

> 'Flee from sexual immorality ... he who sins sexually sins against his own body. Do you not know that your body is a temple of the Holy Spirit, who is in you, whom you have received from God? ... therefore honour God with your body.'
>
> (1 Corinthians 6:18–20)

Now test yourself

5 Why is cyber sex seen by some as immoral?

6 What are the purposes of Christian marriage?

7 What is a civil partnership?

8 Why do some Christians oppose homosexuality?

9 What does it mean to say that the body is a 'temple of the Holy Spirit'?

Answers on page 62

Tested

Moral decision-making
Revised

Today there are widely differing attitudes within sexual ethics – those of religious believers, secular society, parliament, the law, and in moral philosophy. For example:

- Should sexual acts only take place between married couples?
- Should sexual acts be permissible between consenting, unmarried people?
- Should the sexual act involve faithfulness and commitment?
- Is instant pleasure sufficient to justify sexual actions?
- Should adultery be against the law?
- Is homosexuality natural?
- Should homosexuals and heterosexuals have the same rights?

How are these moral questions to be answered? Christianity teaches that:

- Marriage is the relationship that God has established for sexual relationships.
- Other sexual activities such as sex outside marriage, adultery and homosexuality are morally wrong.
- The relationship between sex, marriage and procreation is the most important thing.
- The Church of England's consultative document 'Marriage and the Church's Task' (1978) states: '... love finds expression in the lovers' bodily union ... It is an act of personal commitment which spans past, present and future. It is celebration, healing, renewal, pledge and future. Above all it communicates the affirmation of mutual belonging.'

This has led some churches, perhaps most notoriously the Westboro Baptist Church in the USA, who adopt an absolute ethic position, to campaign vigorously against what they see as sexual immorality, most notably homosexuality.

For secular non-believers, sexual ethics may be viewed in a different way. For example, they may take the libertarian or relative ethical view, which is that sexual relationships are morally permissible if:

- both parties are over the legal age limit
- consent is freely given
- no harm comes to either party
- no deceit is done – no adultery.

The advantage of libertarianism is that it allows consenting adults to do as they please and seems to offer a more tolerant and permissive lifestyle.

Others may prefer the Utilitarian view which is that sexual relations are acceptable as long as:

- they take place in private among consenting adults
- nobody else is offended
- the partners are able to increase their own happiness
- they don't cause emotional harm or deceit, as these relationships lead to greater harm than good.

Yet both the libertarian and Utilitarian views have their weaknesses:

- They do not allow for long-term loving relationships.
- They do not necessarily encourage safe sex.
- Little attention is paid to moral virtues such as faithfulness, commitment and love.

> **Exam practice**
>
> **(a)** Examine the different moral and religious views concerning homosexuality.
>
> **(b)** To what extent are the moral and religious dilemmas surrounding homosexuality resolvable?
>
> **Answer guidance online**
>
> Online

Conclusion

Finding answers to sexual moral dilemmas can be very difficult. Look at the statements below and consider how a religious and a non-religious believer might respond to them:

- Marriage should be for life.
- People who marry in church should not be allowed to divorce.
- A marriage relationship is the best environment for raising children.
- It is too easy to get a divorce nowadays.
- Homosexuals should have the same rights as heterosexuals.
- Sex outside marriage is always wrong.
- Divorce is better than an unhappy marriage.
- Cohabitation is good preparation for marriage.

There are many differing views on sexual attitudes and behaviour today. Some people favour casual or open relationships, others look for love, commitment and faithfulness. Attitudes change all the time, making it difficult to find ethical standards which are acceptable to everyone.

Summary

- ✓ Sexual ethics cause deep concern and division among religious believers.
- ✓ Sex outside marriage is forbidden in scripture, but openly practised in contemporary society.
- ✓ Secular standards of sexual ethics openly conflict with religious standards.
- ✓ The growth of feminism has led to changing attitudes to sexual morality.
- ✓ Divorce has become common in society, yet many religious believers are concerned with this.
- ✓ The Christian church has deep divisions over the issue of homosexuality.
- ✓ Pornography is increasing due to easy access via the Internet.
- ✓ Does religious morality have a place in a liberal secular society?

Now test yourself answers

Area A: Philosophy of Religion

1.1 The Design Argument

Now test yourself

1. **Intelligent design:** The universe shows evidence of having been thought-out in its design.
2. Aquinas believed there was a beneficial order with things working together for a purpose.
3. **Paley's analogy of the watch:** if you found a watch and looked at the way it worked, you would notice intelligent design. The same is true of the working of the universe.
4. **The aesthetic principle:** the beauty of the universe suggests a creator.
5. **Anthropomorphism:** attributing human characteristics to concepts, objects or other animals, in this case, reducing God's characteristics to those of humans.
6. **The analogical argument:** one that uses an analogy between the world and objects of human design.
7. **The anthropic principle:** the physical universe appears to be designed for human life.

1.2 The Cosmological Argument

Now test yourself

1. Necessary being: a being that cannot not exist.
2. Aquinas' Second Way: from cause.
3. **Contingent being:** one which comes in and out of existence.
4. The main principle of the Kalam Argument is that whatever comes into being must have a cause.
5. Craig's main point: that an infinite series of events cannot happen.
6. Hume said we cannot draw conclusions about the universe: it is beyond human experience.
7. McCabe's view: those who are interested in questions about the universe must also be interested in God. By this he means that God and the universe are interrelated and the universe gives us a picture of what God is actually like.
8. Dawkins wanted to depend on science for answers, rather than myths and speculation.

2.1 The problem of evil and suffering

Now test yourself

1. Two examples of moral evil: wrongful human actions such as war and murder.
2. **The inconsistent triad:** the view that God is all-knowing and all-loving, yet evil exists, which is logically inconsistent.
3. Suffering as a test of faith: God allows a person to suffer in order that their faith will grow stronger.
4. **Theodicy:** literally means 'righteous God'. A theodicy is an argument that suggests God is right to allow the existence of evil and suffering because, in some way or another, they are necessary.
5. Augustus said evil came from decisions made by human free-will.
6. Hick.
7. **'Epistemic distance':** the distance God keeps between himself and humanity so that we are not overwhelmed.
8. Evil and suffering can be 'soul making': humans face challenges in order to gain perfection.
9. Whitehead meant that God is part of the universe and can feel the effects of evil and suffering.

2.2 Miracles

Now test yourself

1. 'Interventionalist God': one who, through miracles, gets involved in human affairs.
2. **Natural evil:** natural actions that cause harm such as earthquakes, volcanoes and tsunamis.
3. The principle of testimony: that people tend to tell the truth.
4. A 'strong' miracle is an impossible event.
5. Rudolph Bultmann.
6. Richard Swinburne.
7. Keith Ward.
8. Vardy suggested that miracles were morally incompatible because God helps some people and not others.
9. Hume rejected testimonies because he thought that they were liable to imagine them.
10. Atkins called miracles 'largely pretentious gobbledegook' because he felt that there was no evidence for miracles and that science will one day explain things.

Area B: Ethics

1.1 The relationship between religion and morality

Now test yourself

1. Three viewpoints concerning the relationship between religion and morality:
   (i) morality depends on religion
   (ii) morality is independent of religion
   (iii) morality is opposed to religion.
2. **Divine command ethics:** morality is based on commands given by God.
3. **Categorical imperative:** obeying a moral command out of reason or duty.
4. **Kant's state of ultimate good:** *summum bonum*.
5. Conscience: a gift from God given to all humans.
6. **The Euthyphro Dilemma:** does God command X because it is good, or is X good because God commands it?
7. R. A. Sharpe's criticism is that religious morality was out of date.
8. Nietzsche called religious morality a 'slave morality'.
9. Frederick Copleston said 'the man who loves what is truly good, loves God'.

1.2 Utilitarianism and Situation Ethics

Now test yourself

1. **Act utilitarianism:** acting according to the consequences.
2. **Rule utilitarianism:** acting according to morally correct rules.
3. Remoteness.
4. Does the act make things better or worse?
5. **The 'harm principle':** the majority may only put pressure on the minority if it prevents harm.
6. Give an example of a low pleasure: drunkenness.
7. Give an example of a high pleasure: reading or listening to opera.
8. John Stuart Mill said: 'Better to be Socrates dissatisfied than a pig satisfied'.
9. Joseph Fletcher wrote '*Situation Ethics*'.
10. Doing the most loving thing.
11. St Paul said: 'Love is patient, love is kind'.
12. There are no absolute moral rules that must be obeyed in all situations.
13. Vardy meant that 'personalism' puts people first.

2.1 War and peace

Now test yourself

1. Jesus said: 'All who take up the sword will perish by the sword.'
2. **The economic theory of conflict:** wars begin as disputes over territory or natural resources.
3. **A competent authority:** a legitimate government.
4. Nuclear war has unpredictable consequences and kills innocent civilians.
5. Inner jihad: a personal, spiritual battle.
6. Outer jihad: a war in which Muslims may fight against aggression.
7. Weapons of Mass Destruction.
8. Conrad Grebel.
9. **Conscientious objector:** someone who refuses to fight on grounds of pacifism.
10. Gandhi.

2.2 Sexual ethics

Now test yourself

1. St Paul said that it is 'better to marry than burn with passion'.
2. The libertarian view: that sex between those of legal age and consent is acceptable.
3. The Utilitarian view: that sex between consenting people in private is acceptable as long as nobody is harmed.
4. When women are free from male dominance.
5. Cyber sex is seen by some as immoral because those involved are seen not as human individuals, but as sex objects.
6. The purposes of Christian marriage are companionship, love and procreation.
7. **A civil partnership:** a legal agreement between two people that they will share their lives together.
8. It goes against God's will and is regarded by some as unnatural.
9. Life is a creation of God and that God dwells within each person.

Exam practice answer guidance at **www.therevisionbutton.co.uk/myrevisionnotes**

Glossary

A posteriori An argument based on the evidence of our observation of the world.

Actuality What does happen.

Adultery Having sex with someone when you are married to someone else.

Aesthetic principle The idea that the beauty in the world is proof of intelligent design.

Agape God's love for humanity.

Analogical An argument based on analogies or similarities, for example, seeing the link between the world and objects of human design.

Anthropic principle The idea that the world was designed to support human life.

Anthropomorphism The act of attributing human characteristics to concepts, objects or other animals.

Big Bang theory The view that the universe developed from rapid heating and cooling, which led to the formation of matter.

Categorical imperative Obeying a moral command out of reason or duty.

Celibate Not having sex as a devotion to God.

Chastity Not having sex for personal reasons.

Complete explanation One which explains all the factors are to which nothing more can be added.

Consequentialist theory The right thing depends on the consequences and end result.

Contingent being One which comes in and out of existence or need not have existed, e.g. a human being.

Counter-factual hypotheses If God interferes, then humanity cannot develop.

Cyber sex Sexual activity through the internet via computers and other technologies.

Demythologise Taking away the fictional stories in the scripture, leaving only the spiritual truths behind.

Divine command ethics Morality is based on commands given by God.

Empirical Using evidence gained from the senses: touch, smell, sight, taste and sound.

Epistemic distance God keeps a distance from humanity in order not to overwhelm.

Euthyphro Dilemma Does God command what is good or is it good because God commands it?

Fidelity Love and trust for each other.

Hedonic Calculus This involves Calculating the amount of pleasure by considering seven key factors about the practical application of pleasure.

Inconsistent triad God is all-loving and all-powerful, yet evil exists.

Inductive An argument based on premises and conclusions, for example, the universe shows order and therefore must have been designed.

Infinite chain of movers A line of movers that goes back forever, without beginning or end.

Inner jihad A personal spiritual battle.

Intelligent design The universe shows evidence of having been thought-out in its design.

Interventionalist God, through miracles, intervenes in human affairs.

Jihad Holy war in Islam.

Jus ad bellum Resort to war.

Jus in bello Conduct in war.

Just War A war which religious believers may fight under certain conditions.

Libertarian view Sexual relationships are morally permissible.

Moral evil The results of human action such as murder or theft.

Natural evil Problems in the natural world, which lead to tsunamis, earthquakes and famines.

Natural laws The laws of nature, upon which science is based, that govern the way the universe seems to operate.

Natural selection The biological process by which certain animals become more or less common due to genetic characteristics and changes.

Necessary being A being that must exist and cannot not exist.

Necessary cause A cause that cannot not exist.

Outer jihad Where Muslims fight against oppression.

Potentiality What might happen.

Procreation Having children.

Relativistic moral theory Where there are no absolute moral rules.

Secular Belonging to the world, rather than religion.

Summum bonum The state of ultimate or greatest good.

Teleological theory Truth is discovered through nature and purpose.

Theodicy Literally 'righteous God'. A theodicy is an argument that suggests God is right to allow the existence of evil and suffering because, in some way or another, they are necessary.

Universal ethical hedonism Everyone has an equal right to happiness.